# Software Testing and Global Industry

# Software Testing and Global Industry: Future Paradigms

By

Valentine Casey

Editors

Ita Richardson and Míchéal Ó hAodha

CAMBRIDGE SCHOLARS

PUBLISHING

Software Testing and Global Industry: Future Paradigms, by Valentine Casey
Editors: Ita Richardson and Míchéal Ó hAodha

This book first published 2009

Cambridge Scholars Publishing

12 Back Chapman Street, Newcastle upon Tyne, NE6 2XX, UK

British Library Cataloguing in Publication Data
A catalogue record for this book is available from the British Library



ISBN (10): 1-4438-0109-7, ISBN (13): 978-1-4438-0109-6

This book is dedicated to my wife Gloria without whose love,
encouragement and continuous support this project
could not have been carried out.

# TABLE OF CONTENTS

# PREFACE

The advent of low-cost telecommunications coupled with the availability of well-educated low-cost labour in developing countries has made the implementation of a Global Software Development strategy popular with many software development companies in recent years. While the argument for doing this is often financial, other benefits include access to a technical labour force, proximity to a customer market and the possibility of setting-up 24-hour development cycles around the world. Although more and more companies implement Global Software Development, oftentimes, from a variety of perspectives, the strategy is not fully thought through. In fact, where companies implement Global Software Development solely from a financial perspective, they can be surprised at the 'real' implementation costs. Furthermore, while such a strategy may be to the benefit of a company, it may not be of benefit to the individual employees. They often have to cope with changing working conditions and possibly job losses in the longer term.

The discussion in this book focuses on a U.S. multi-national company who outsourced testing from its subsidiary in Ireland using virtual teams and the circumstances surrounding the implementation of the teams. The techniques used to collect the data include 5-months participant-observation followed by interviews with the software engineers who were based in Ireland. Analysis of this data resulted in the presentation of factors which managers should consider when implementing a Global Software Development strategy if it is to be successful.

**Dr. Ita Richardson, Head of Operations – (Lero - the Irish Software Engineering Research Centre**

# ACKNOWLEDGEMENTS

This research was supported by the Science Foundation Ireland funded project, Global Software Development in Small to Medium Sized Enterprises (GSD for SMEs) grant number 03/IN3/1408C within Lero - the Irish Software Engineering Research Centre (http://www.lero.ie) and by Principal Investigator grant number 02/IN.1/I108.

# CHAPTER ONE

# GLOBAL SOFTWARE DEVELOPMENT

## 1. Globalisation

The last two decades have witnessed an escalating trend toward the globalisation of business. This has led to the advent of a radically different global economic environment and new methods of operation. As a result, organisations are now operating in a truly global environment. Doing business in this environment is increasingly challenging. While there are more business opportunities than ever before, there is also much more competition.[1] This competition is coming from low-cost production centres with skilled workforces producing quality products. Until recently, the West's strategic economic advantage lay in its use of technology and its effective production methods. These factors were capitalised upon by a well-educated work force which could utilise these factors to maximise the competitive advantage they offered.

The advent of globalisation has meant that the old methods of achieving and maintaining competitive advantage are no longer as effective as they once were.[2] Goods can now be produced to the same level of quality and at a much cheaper price in more low-cost economies. To survive in this increasingly competitive economic environment companies are adapting their products and manufacturing locations to compete and capitalise on the opportunities which the global market provides. This has led to the

---

1 Turban, E., R.K. Rainer, Jr., and E.R. Potter, Introduction to Information Technology. Second ed. 2003: John Wiley & Sons, Inc.

2 Grenier, R. and G. Metes, Going Virtual: Moving Your Organization in to the 21st Century. 1995, Upper Saddle River, NJ: Prentice Hall; Yager, S.E., Everything's Coming Up Virtual. Crossroads: Special issue on interdisciplinary computer science, 1997. 4(1): p. 20 - 24.; Davidow, W.H. and M.S. Malone, The Virtual Corporation. 1992, New York: Edward Brulingame Books/Harper Business.

relocation of manufacturing operations to countries such as Mexico, and other locations in Latin America, Eastern Europe and the Far East.[3]

A positive aspect of this development has been the expansion of world markets. As less-developed countries have benefited from increased economic prosperity, sections of their population have also been able to enhance their purchasing power. This has resulted in increased international demand for products and services. Those countries who have reaped the economic benefits of globalisation have also invested in their internal infrastructure and their education systems in order to support, maintain and expand their economic growth.[4]

One of the major outcomes of globalisation has been the loss of low-skilled manufacturing jobs in Western economies. On the positive side, these jobs have been replaced by more value-added type positions which utilise the advantages that high skill levels and location can provide. Furthermore, the loss of large numbers of low-skilled type positions as provided an incentive for students in these countries to attain higher academic and technical qualifications, thereby gaining additional value-added skills.[5]

## 1.1 Software Globalisation

The advent of the Internet, e-mail, intranets, extranets and improved low-cost international telecommunications has facilitated the development of virtual work groups and virtual companies.[6] These developments in communication have had a particular impact in the software industry. Such factors have been instrumental in instigating the migration of software development and maintenance operations to more geographically-

---

[3] Miller, D.S., S.E. Catt, and J.R. Carlson, Fundamentals of Management: A Framework for Excellence. 1996, St Paul, MN: West Publishing Company.
[4] Lipnack, J. and J. Stamp, Virtual Teams: Reaching Across Space, Time And Originating With Technology. 1997: John Wiley and Sons.
[5] Gopal, A., T. Mukhopadhyay, and M.S. Krishnan, The Role of Software Process and Communication in Offshore Software Development. Communicatications of the ACM, 2002. 45(4): p. 193-200.
[6] Crow, G. and B. Muthuswamy, International Outsourcing in the Information Technology Industry: Trends and Implications. Communications of the International Information Management Association, 2003 3(1): p. 25 - 34.

distributed locations.[7] In some cases, applications development and maintenance has been completely outsourced to remote third-party organisations. In other cases, multinational organisations have set up subsidiaries in low-cost economies. In the software sector, such approaches are known as Distributed Software Development, (DSD), Global Distribution of Software (GDS) or Global Software Development (GSD). The utilisation of such approaches has increased in popularity and has become an important strategy for the software industry generally.

Initially, the trend was for organisations to outsource basic software application development and maintenance activities to third parties or subsidiaries based in countries such as Ireland and India. In the beginning, these included projects such as Y2K and other projects incorporating straightforward development and maintenance. As a result of the success which this approach achieved, the level of confidence in this strategy has increased and organisations are now off-shoring or outsourcing more complex and mission-critical development projects. All of these factors have led to the situation today whereby software development has become a globally-sourced commodity

The dynamic nature of GSD is highlighted by the fact that the focus for off-shoring and outsourcing activities has shifted away from Ireland over the last few years. Nowadays many Irish-based multinationals and indigenous organisations are outsourcing and off-shoring their software development. This strategic change can be directly attributed to the country's economic success which has resulted in increased development costs.[8] Having achieved considerable success in the IT sector, the focus of the software industry in Ireland is now moving towards value-added (niche) and research-and- development-centric strategies. However, outsourcing and off-shoring sectors continue to expand in Eastern Europe, India and other locations in the Far East.

The general view is that organisations which implement a globally distributed software development strategy are increasingly seeking to gain

---

[7] Hayes, I.S., Ready or Not: Global Sourcing Is in Your IT Future. Cutter IT Journal, 2002. 15(11): p. 5 - 11.

[8] Cusumano, M.A., Software in Ireland: a balance of entrepreneurship and…lifestyle management? Communications of the ACM, 2005. 48 (10 ): p. 25 - 27.

a competitive advantage.[9] This development is attributed to labour arbitrage which is facilitated by the availability of large numbers of well-educated and technically competent software engineers in Eastern Europe, India and the Far East.[10] It is also believed that this can provide the opportunity for a shorter development cycle due to the leveraging of the temporal differences between the local site and the offshored or outsourced locations. The adoption of this approach facilitates the implementation of what has been termed a '*follow the sun'* development strategy.[11]

In these circumstances, the prospects for the availability of a large low-cost labour pool with the required skill-set is very attractive.[12] Coupled with the opportunity for round-the-clock development, these factors are all strong driving forces for the adoption of a GSD strategy[13]. In the majority of situations where GSD is implemented, the motivation is to leverage these various potential advantages so as to be the first to market and/or become a competitive player. The overall objective is to enable organisations to gain, maintain or increase their market share in what has become an increasingly volatile and dynamic global business environment.[14]

Given the potential economic benefits afforded by implementing this approach, the current trend to globalise software development is set to continue for the foreseeable future. This trend is further illustrated by the fact that Indian software companies are now outsourcing projects to China, Vietnam, and the Philippines. The number of organisations globalising

---

[9] Prikladnicki, R., J.L.N. Audy, and R. Evaristo, Global software development in practice lessons learned Software Process Improvement and Practice 2003. 8(4): p. 267 - 279.

[10] Toaff, S.S., Don't Play with "Mouths of Fire," and Other Lessons of Global Software Development. Cutter IT Journal, 2002. 15(11): p. 23 - 28.

[11] Carmel, E., Global Software Teams: Collaboration Across Borders and Time Zones. 1999, Saddle River, NJ: Prentice Hall.

[12] Carmel, E. and R. Agarwal, Tactical Approaches for Alleviating Distance in Global Software Development. IEEE Software, 2001. 1(2): p. 22 - 29; Ebert, C. and P. De Neve, Surviving Global Software Development. IEEE Software, 2001. 18(2): p. 62 - 69.

[13] Edwards, H.K. and V. Sridhar. Analysis of the effectiveness of global virtual teams in software engineering projects. in The 36th Hawaii International Conference on System Sciences. 2003. Hawaii.

[14] Lipnack, J. and J. Stamp, Virtual Teams: People Working Across Boundaries with Technology. 2nd ed. 2000, New York: John Wiley & Sons. Inc.

their software development continues to rise. Ultimately, this means that globally distributed software development is set to have a significant ongoing impact on the software industry and the world economy as a whole.

### 1.1.1 Manufacturing versus Global Software Development

While global manufacturing has been a very successful phenomenon, the experience gained in other distributed development environments does not easily transfer to the software industry. This can be attributed to the levels of complexity involved in software development[15] including such issues as the problem of understanding requirements and integration. These difficulties are further compounded by cultural, linguistic and temporal differences, a lack of communication, manufacturer-customer distance and diverse process-maturity levels, testing tools, standards, technical ability and experience. These all have a strong impact particularly given that software development is a people-centric rather than a machine-centric activity. It is therefore vital that those involved in global software development have a good awareness of the organisational, motivational, cultural and communication-related issues that arise throughout the software life cycle.

## 1.2 Software Project Management

An essential element for the successful development of software is effective project management[16]. Software project management has been defined in the following terms:

> "Software project management today is an art. The skillful integration of software technology, economics and human relations in the specific context of a software project is not an easy task. The software project is a highly people-intensive effort that spans a very lengthy period, with fundamental implications on the work and performance of many different classes of people".[17]

---

[15] Brooks, F.P., No Silver Bullet: Essence and Accidents of Software Engineering Computer, 1987. 20(4): p. 10 -19.

[16] Van Vliet, H., Software Engineering : Principles and Practice. 2nd ed. 2000, Chichester, U.K.: Wiley.

[17] Boehm, B.W. and R. Ross, Theory-W Software Project Management Principles And Examples. IEEE Transactions on Engineering Management, 1989. 15(7): p. 902 – 916.

The role of the software Project Manager can be compared to that of a juggler.[18] There is the need to be an arbitrator between diverse stakeholders with different expectations and agendas. There is also the requirement to manage the operation of the team effectively within the constraints of available resources, both financial and technological. The latter has to be achieved utilising the personnel and technical capabilities that are then available. The responsibility of the software Project Manager is to determine these various objectives. It is also the Project Manager's responsibility to define, create, evaluate and select alternatives in order to achieve these objectives and to control their implementation.[19] This is accomplished through planning, organising, staffing, leading, controlling and coordinating the project in an effective manner[20].

This range of characteristics is not adequate on its own, however. They also need to be coupled with the ability to plan, estimate, monitor and control the project effectively. The Project Manager needs to have the ability to arbitrate, appease, admonish, praise, inspire and motivate those whom they manage, often across a range of globally-distributed team-based projects. To summarise the software project management role: it requires effective people management, business management, risk management, and expectation management. Operating in a globally distributed environment, project management becomes a more complex task to undertake than in a collocated project.[21]

Therefore, it is no surprise that, in addition to the necessity for the effective organisation and management of collocated teams and projects, there are additional issues which require consideration in relation to the operation of geographically-distributed teams and their related projects.

---

[18] Wiegers, K.E., 21 Project Management Success Tips, in Software Management D.J. Reifer, Editor. 2002, IEEE Computer Society: Los Alamitos, Calif. USA. p. 171 - 181.

[19] Gilb, T. and S. Finz, Principles of Software Engineering Management 1988, Wokingham, U.K.: Addison-Wesley.

[20] Weihrich, H., Management: Science, Thoery and Practice in Software Engineering Project Management, R.H. Thayer, Editor. 2000, IEEE Computer Society Press,: Los Alamitos, Ca. USA. p. 4 – 13; Reifer, D.J., Traditional Software Management Approaches, in Software Management, D.J. Reifer, Editor. 2002, IEEE Computer Society: Los Alamitos, Calif. USA. p. 137 – 148; Summerville, I., Software Engineering, ed. t. Edition. 2001, Harlow UK: Pearson Education Ltd.

[21] Karolak, D.W., Global Software Development: Managing Virtual Teams and Environments. 1999, Los Alamitos, CA, USA IEEE Computer Society Press.

> "The complex, usually uncertain, and highly interdependent nature of project tasks, together with geographical, temporal, structural and cultural gaps fundamental to distributed teams, make management of virtual projects a relatively complex undertaking".[22]

All these different factors, issues and variables need to be specifically addressed in a globally distributed team environment.

Effective communication and project management skills are essential in large collocated software development projects.[23] There are more important issues still for the operation of globally distributed software development.[24] The negative impact of distance on communication and coordination is well-documented.[25] Research has shown that cross-site communication and coordination negatively impacts on the speed of distributed software development.[26] The importance of good communication[27] and effective project management[28] cannot be

---

[22] Paré, G. and L. Dubé. Virtual teams: an exploratory study of key challenges and strategies in Proceeding of the 20th the International Conference on Information Systems 1999 Charlotte, North Carolina, United States: Association for Information Systems.

[23] Curtis, B., H. Krasner, and N. Iscoe, A Field Study Of The Software Design Process For Large Systems. Communications of the ACM, 1988 31(11): p. 1268 – 1287.

[24] Battin, R.D., et al., Leveraging Resources in Global Software Development. IEEE Software, 2001. 1(2): p. 70 – 77; Rutkowski, A.F., et al., E-collaboration: The Reality of Virtuality. IEEE Transactions on Professional Communication, 2002. 45 (4): p. 219 – 230; Beise, C.M. IT Project Management And Virtual Teams. in Proceedings of the 2004 SIGMIS conference on Computer personnel research: Careers, culture, and ethics in a networked environment 2004. Tucson, AZ, USA ACM Press.

[25] Herbsleb, J.D., et al. An Empirical Study of Global Software Development: Distance and Speed. in Proceedings of the 23rd International Conference on Software Engineering, 2001. ICSE 2001. 2001 Toronto, Canada; Ebert, C., et al. Improving validation activities in a global software development in Proceedings of the 23rd International Conference on Software Engineering 2001 Toronto, Ontario, Canada IEEE Computer Society.

[26] Herbsleb, J.D., et al. Distance, Dependencies and Delay in Global Collaboration. in Proceedings of the 2000 ACM conference on Computer supported cooperative work 2000. Philadelphia, Pennsylvania, USA ACM Press.

[27] Suchan, J. and G. Hayzak, The communication characteristics of virtual teams: A case study. IEEE Transactions on Professional Communication,, 2001. 44(3): p. 174-186.

[28] Nidiffer, K.E. and D. Dolan, Evolving distributed project management. IEEE Software 2005. 22(5): p. 63 – 72.

underestimated in the context of effective globally distributed team operation.

### 1.2.1 Project Management in The GSD Environment

The impact of a distributed environment on the project management of GSD teams is considerable. The essence of effective management is coordination and control. Distance introduces complexity which directly impacts on both coordination and control and the facilitation of communication.[29] It is also affected by the level of project visibility which can be negatively impacted by distance. This range of variables is also influenced by language, culture and work processes. The need for effective collaboration and visibility between locations is essential.

All of these factors have a direct influence on the level of cooperation which can be achieved. An overview of the distance issue and its impact on the operation of globally distributed teams is presented in Figure 1.1.

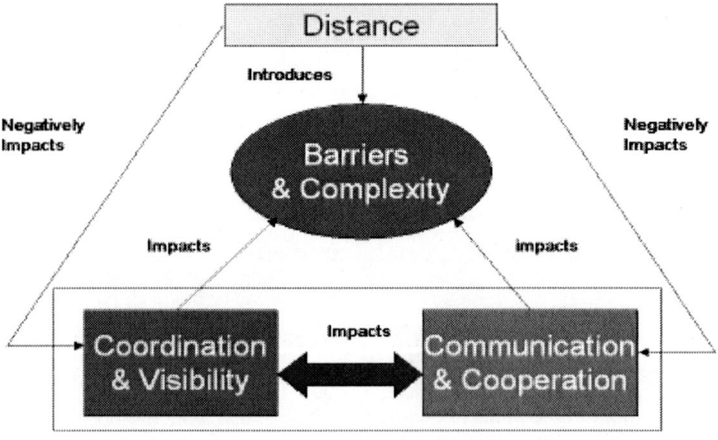


Figure 1.1: The Impact Of Distance On The Operation of Globally Distributed Teams

[29] Herbsleb, J.D. and A. Mockus, An Empirical Study of Speed and Communication in Globally Distributed Software Development IEEE Transactions on Software Engineering, 2003. 29(6): p. 481-494; Damian, D.E. and D. Zowghi. An insight into the interplay between culture, conflict and distance in globally distributed requirements negotiations. in Proceedings of the 36th International Conference on Systems Sciences (HICSS'03). IEEE. 2002. 2003. Hawaii.

This makes managing a global software team very difficult. Carmel (1999) paraphrased the particular difficulties faced by a software manager when he stated that *"no one in their right mind would do this"*. However, globally distributed software projects have to be managed effectively. Carmel (1999) identifies coordination breakdown as one of the five centrifugal forces which negatively impacts on the effective operation of globally distributed teams. His other four forces are loss of team-work, cultural difference, geographical dispersion and loss of communication richness. Carmel has also outlined six centripetal forces which can be utilised to counterbalance these issues. They are managerial techniques, team building, product architecture, telecoms infrastructure, collaborative technology and development methodology. The causes of the various problems experienced in effectively managing a globally disturbed team have been identified as follows:

> "Notably, globally distributed teams must contend with difficulties in communication and coordination that arise from differences in time zones, geographical location, and culture".[30]

## 1.3 Team Motivation And Trust

Effective planning, coordination, control and communication are essential aspects of effective project management for collocated and globally distributed software developments. To undertake these activities successfully, due consideration needs to be given to people management. Motivation and the development of trust are essential for effective people management[31] particularly in a GSD team environment.[32] In this context, it was considered of value to consider the literature on motivation.

### 1.3.1 Motivation

---

[30] Davidson, E.J. and A.S.M. Tay. Studying Teamwork in Global IT Support in In the Proceedings of the 36th Hawaii International Conference on Systems Science. 2003. Kona-Kailua, HI.

[31] Dawson, S., Analysing Organisations. 1992, London, UK: The Macmillan Press Ltd.; Handy, C.B., Understating Organizations. 1985, London, UK: Penguin Books.

[32] Casey, V. and I. Richardson. Practical Experience of Virtual Team Software Development. in Euro SPI 2004 European Software Process Improvement. 2004. Trondheim, Norway.

In his seminal works "*A Theory of Human Motivation*"[33] and "*Motivation and Personality*"[34], Abraham Maslow presented what has become known as Maslow's Hierarchy of Needs (see Figure 1.2). He proposed that humans have five types of needs, as organised in a hierarchical format. This group is further divided into what are termed lower-level '*deficiency*' needs, (or basic needs) and the higher-level '*being*' needs (or growth needs).

The deficiency needs are defined as:

- **Physiological needs**. Which Maslow refers to as homeostasis. These are the basic requirements for survival. These needs are the functioning of the body, the consumption of food, water, air etc. The greatest desire is to satisfy these needs and they take priority over all others until they are satisfied.

- **Safety needs.** When the physiological needs are met the individual has the desire to feel safe and secure.

- **Social needs**. When the physiological and safety needs are addressed the individual's desire is for social relationships. Humans have a need to be loved, to be accepted and to be a part of a group.

---

[33] Maslow, A.H., A Theory Of Human Motivation. Psychological Review, 1943. 50: p. 370 - 396.
[34] Maslow, A.H., Motivation and Personality 2nd ed. 1970, New York, USA: Harper and Row.

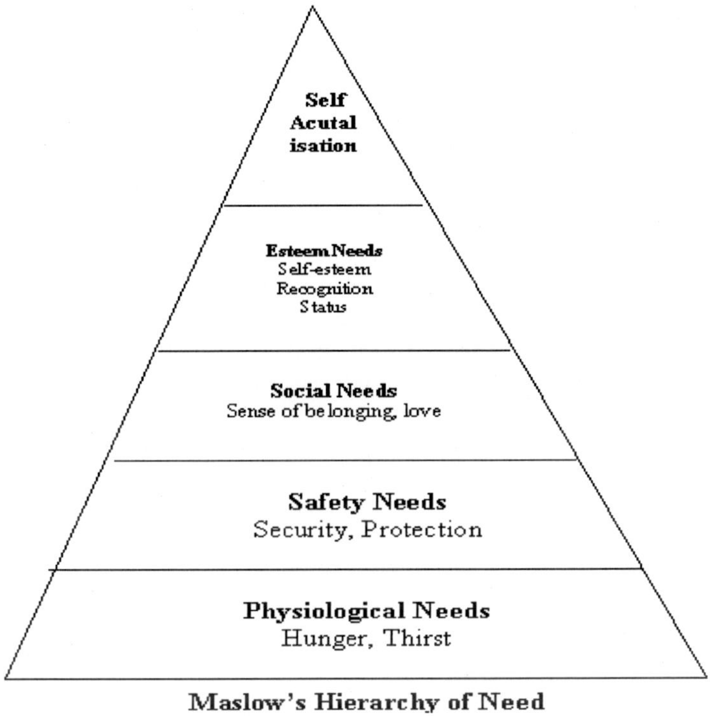


Figure 1.2

The term 'deficiency needs' is derived from the view that, if an individual is deficient in the areas of basic physiological, safety and social needs, they will fail to develop into a healthy person, both physically and psychologically. Maslow's view is that the individual is motivated to fulfil these primary needs in the order they are presented. This must take place prior to fulfilling what are termed the higher order 'being' needs.

The 'being' needs are defined as:

- **Esteem needs**. All individuals have a desire for self respect or, as Maslow calls it - *self-esteem* and the respect of others.

- **Self-actualisation**. Once the esteem needs are met, the individual has the desire for self-fulfilment. Maslow defines self actualisation as *"The tendency might be phrased as the desire to become more*

> *and more what one is, to become everything that one is capable of becoming*".

The 'being' needs (or growth needs) allow the individual to grow and achieve their full potential.

Based on the five needs or goals outlined, the individual is motivated to achieve or maintain their level of satisfaction in order to address these needs. Maslow has defined these as the key human motivating factors and in his view the individual is constantly striving to satisfy these goals. Given the hierarchical order of these needs, the individual is centrally focused on the achievement of each level sequentially. This is to the exclusion of those needs placed above those currently desired. Once the individual's current needs are met, the higher needs are then focused on, the premise being that once the needs at one level are satisfied that they are no longer motivators. The value of such a hierarchy of needs is that, if a person's location can be determined on the scale, the effective motivating factors can also be identified.

While Maslow's work was the basis for much subsequent further research, it is not without its critics. "*There is very little empirical support for his view of a universal hierarchy*". There is also the view that there very limited evidence exists that needs are activated in the order which Maslow postulates.[35] Additional research has been carried out by Clayton Alderfer, research which goes some way towards addressing these issues. Alderfer has developed what is call based on Maslow's Hierarchy of Needs, ed ERG theory[36], where he outlines three types of human needs:

- **E**xistence
- **R**elatedness
- **G**rowth

The term *Existence* equates with Maslow's physiological and safety needs. *Relatedness* links to the individual's requirement for social relationships while *Growth* relates to the human need for esteem and self-actualisation. These three concepts encompass Maslow's five areas of needs.

---

[35] Furnham, A., The Psychology of Behaviour at Work: The individual in the organisation. 1997, Hove, East Sussex, UK: Psychology Press.

[36] Alderfer, C.P., Existence Relatedness and Growth: Human Needs in Organizational Settings. 1972, New York: Free Press.

Where Alderfer differs from Maslow is in his view that these needs do not need satisfying in any particular order and that more than one single set of needs may be influential at any particular time. He suggests that if a high-level need cannot be satisfied, the individual's desire to address a lower level need is increased as a consequence. This he identifies as the "*frustration and shy aggression dimension*". A constituent element of this approach is the organisational setting wherein an employee can have multiple needs to satisfy simultaneously.

### 1.3.2 Motivation: Theory X And Theory Y

Given the importance of motivation, it should be considered when selecting an effective management strategy. Douglas McGregor in his Theory X and Theory Y outlined two opposing views of management's approach to motivation. His work was based on Maslow's hierarchy of needs and he separates the lower-order needs into what he terms Theory X and the higher-order needs into Theory Y. A key element of McGregor's approach is *"Behind every managerial decision or action are assumptions about human nature and human behaviour".*[37] This statement is a key element in his Theory X and Theory Y approach to management.

**Theory X**: the traditional view of direction and control, as McGregor defines it, is based on three managerial assumptions with regard to workers and how they operate:

1. The normal worker dislikes work and will avoid it if he can.
2. Workers must be coerced, controlled, threatened and directed to put forth the required effort to achieve the organisation's objectives.
3. The normal worker wishes to be directed, likes to avoid responsibility, wants security and has little ambition.

The negative assumptions regarding the characteristics of employees as outlined in the Theory X style of management ensures that motivation is authoritarian and is supported by the threat of punishment for non-compliance. McGregor locates the roots of Theory X in the biblical view of Adam and the Fall whereby mankind was forced '*to earn his bread by the sweat of his brow'*. McGregor sums this up as follows: "*Theory X*

---

[37] McGregor, D., The Human Side of Enterprise 1960 New York, Toronto, London.: McGraw-Hill Book Company, Inc.

*explains the consequences of a particular management strategy: it neither explains nor describes human nature although it purports to*".[38]

In contrast, Theory Y - the integration of individual and organisational goals - is based on six managerial assumptions regarding workers:

1. Individuals do not dislike work and it is as natural to them as play or rest.
2. People are not lazy. Control and the threat of punishment are not the only methods that can be used to motivate staff and to achieve organisational goals. When an individual is committed to the achievement of an objective they will exercise self-direction and self-control to achieve that end.
3. Commitment to objectives is a function of the reward associated with their achievement. Self-actualisation can be a direct result of the effort expended in achieving organisational objectives.
4. Individuals working under proper conditions not only learn to accept responsibility but also come to welcome it. The desire to avoid responsibility, a lack of ambition and a focus on security are not inherited human characteristics, but factors which are learned over time.
5. Large numbers of people can exercise a level of imagination, creativity and ingenuity in their approach to solving organisational problems.
6. In industry, only part of the intellectual potential of the individual is utilised.

The Theory Y style of management assumes that individuals enjoy work, are self-motivated and self-controlled. They welcome responsibility and can be creative and imaginative in their approach to problem solving. There is also a pool of unutilised potential which can be harnessed for greater productivity, if employees are given the opportunity to excel. The satisfaction of doing a good job is an effective motivator rather than the "*carrot and stick approach*". The focus of a Theory Y manager is to remove the barriers which may prevent their staff from achieving their full potential.

---

[38] McGregor, D., The Human Side of Enterprise 1960 New York, Toronto, London.: McGraw-Hill Book Company, Inc.

### 1.3.3 Trust

A lack of trust has been identified as a consequence of globally distributed software development.[39] The establishment of trust in a globally distributed team environment is therefore an important endeavour.

Charles Handy, when discussing trust in the virtual organisation outlines seven cardinal principles of trust[40]:

1. **Trust is not blind.** Handy asserts that it is difficult for workers to build a sense of trust with people who are not well known to them. Similarly, he states it is ill-advised to trust people who have not been observed over a period of time and who do not share the same goals and objectives as others.

2. **Trust requires boundaries.** Unlimited trust is not practical or unrealistic. In the organisational sense, trust equates to confidence in someone's ability and their commitment to common goals.

3. **Trust demands learning**. There is a need for organisational flexibility and the organisation, as a whole, needs to learn how to address problems associated with the operation of virtual teams.

4. **Trust is tough.** People must be up to doing the job. They must earn trust and if, after all the training and support is given, it does not work out, then alternative individuals or strategies have to be adopted.

5. **Trust needs bonding**. This is particularly relevant in the virtual environment where distance, in all its forms, directly conspires to prevent bonding taking place. Rather than being self-contained

---

[39] Herbsleb, J.D. and D. Moitra, Global Software Development. IEEE Software, 2001. 18(2): p. 16 - 20; Damian, D. and D. Zowghi, Requirments Engineering Challenges in Multi-Site Software Development Organizations. Requirements Engineering 2003. 8: p. 149-160; Oppenheimer, H.L. Project Management Issues in Globally Distributed Development in ICSE Workshop on Global Software Development. 2002.

[40] Handy, C., Trust and the Virtual Organization. Harvard Business Review, 1995. 73(3): p. 40 -40.

individual units, the elements of a virtual team need to gel into a single team.

6. **Trust requires keeping in touch.** In Handy's view, personal contact is vital. "*The more virtual an organisation becomes the more people need to meet face to face*".[41]

7. **Trust requires leadership.** When a team trust each other, they are focused on the achievement of a common goal. They do not see each other as opponents; instead, they are comrades in the attainment of a common objective. This level of trust comes from a confidence in good leadership and in each other. A good leader fosters and develops that confidence

## 1.4 Communication

Effective communication is a vital process in every organisation and is defined as: "*Any behaviour that results in an exchange of meaning or mutual exchange of facts, thoughts, opinions or emotions*".[42] Communication is widely recognised as being central to the individual and to organisational performance. In these circumstances, the need for effective communication cannot be underestimated. Without effective communication, a successful business cannot operate. *"Management is communication. Every managerial function and activity involves some form of direct or indirect communication".*[43] It has been acknowledged that good communication is essential for the operation of organisations with an integrated collocated structure. It is also well documented that even in this setting communication problems can and do arise.[44]

The importance of good team communication in software development has been well documented. In these circumstances, it is no surprise that effective communication is an important issue for organisations implementing a GSD virtual team strategy. This fact is highlighted by this

---

[41] Handy, C., Trust and the Virtual Organization. Harvard Business Review, 1995. 73(3): p. 40 -40.
[42] Rollinson, D., A. Broadfield, and D.J. Edwards, Organisational Behaviour and Analysis: An Integrated Approach. 1998, UK: Addison-Wesley.
[43] Kreitner, R., A. Kinicki, and M. Buelens, Organizational Behaviour First European Edition ed. 1999, London UK McGraw-Hill Publishing Company.
[44] Martin, J., Organizational behaviour 1997 London: International Thomson Business.

definition of the virtual team: "*Unlike conventional teams, a virtual team works across space, time, and organizational boundaries with links strengthened by webs of communication technologies*".[45] In the globally distributed virtual team environment, distance impacts negatively on the effectiveness of communication. "*Potentially the largest source of problems in GSD are issues related to communication across sites*".[46] The reasons for the negative impact distance has on communication are well documented. They include geographical, temporal and cultural distance, language differences and the necessity for reliance on asynchronous communication tools.[47]

## 1.5 Culture

The research literature has identified the importance of culture as a factor impacting on globally distributed software development[48] and on the operation of virtual software teams, in particular. The multidimensional effects which culture has on GSD projects has been documented.[49] Its full implications are highlighted by the fact that cultural differences have been

---

[45] Crow, G. and B. Muthuswamy, International Outsourcing in the Information Technology Industry: Trends and Implications. Communications of the International Information Management Association, 2003 3(1): p. 25 - 34.
[46] Mockus, A. and J.D. Herbsleb. Challenges of global software development. in Proceedings. Seventh International Software Metrics Symposium, 2001. 2001. London, UK.
[47] Boland, D. and B. Fitzgerald. Transitioning from a Co-Located to a Globally-Distributed Software Development Team: A Case Study at Analog Devices Inc. in Proc. of the International Workshop on GSD, international Conference on Software Engineering (ICSE 2004). 2004. Edinburgh, Scotland.
Herbsleb, J.D. and R.E. Grinter. Splitting the Organization and Integrating the Code: Conway's Law Revisited. in 21st International Conference on Software Engineering. 1999. Los Angeles, California, United States: IEEE Computer Society Press.
Kiel, L. Experiences in Distributed Development: A Case Study. in International Workshop on Global Software Development,. 2003. Portland, Oregon, USA.
[48] Krishna, S., S. Sahay, and G. Walsham, Managing cross-cultural issues in global software outsourcing Communications of the ACM, 2004. 47 (4): p. 62 - 66.
[49] Evaristo, J.R. and R. Scudder. Geographically distributed project teams: a dimensional analysis. in Proceedings of the 33rd Annual Hawaii International Conference on System Sciences, 2000. 2000. Hawaii.
Olson, J.S. and G.M. Olson, Culture Surprises in Remote Software Development Teams Queue ACM Press, 2003. 1(9): p. 52 - 59.

identified as one of the five centripetal forces which negatively impact on global software teams.

Culture is manifested in two ways within organisations. One is the effect of organisational culture and the other is the impact of national culture. Organisational or corporate culture has been defined as "*shared values and beliefs, which are seen to characterise particular organisations*".[50] National culture has been described in terms of shared values, beliefs and philosophies that affect the way society is organised. These values, norms and beliefs are shaped by a common history, tradition, climate and prosperity.[51]

All culture is acquired through socialisation and organisations may work to achieve a corporate culture. Some multinational organisations have a corporate strategy that enforces standard décor, procedures, stationary and a dress code policy as applied across its worldwide operation. Whilst this standardisation is at a cosmetic level, it does nevertheless help to reinforce the corporate culture. Corporate norms, beliefs, values and objectives are imparted though training, management style, communication methods, rewards and organisational structure. How effective the transmission of the organisational culture is depends on the difference between its values and norms and the national culture of those whom it is being imparted to. While there may be an outward compliance, national culture is always difficult to change and this can only effectively take place over an extended time period.[52]

There is a need for organisations not only to learn and understand the customs and courtesies of their remote staff, but also to understand their national character, their business philosophy and their mindset.[53] It is in this context that the literature is presented here and the research is discussed with reference to some later findings as discussed in Chapter six.

---

[50] Handy, C., Trust and the Virtual Organization. Harvard Business Review, 1995. 73(3): p. 40 -40.
[51] Handy, C., Trust and the Virtual Organization. Harvard Business Review, 1995. 73(3): p. 40 -40.
[52] Hall, W., Managing cultures: making strategic relationships work. 1995, Chichester, England: Wiley.
[53] Harris, P.R. and R.T. Moran, Managing Cultural Differences: Leadership Stategies for a New World of Business. 4th ed. 1996, Houston, USA: Gulf Publishing Company.

### 1.5.1 The Dimensions of Culture

Given the nature of this research, one of the most relevant classifications of culture is that derived by Geert Hofstede[54], a definition which was based on research carried out in the International Business Machines (IBM) Corporation between 1967 and 1973. At the time, IBM was one of the largest multinational companies in the world.[55] This research had focused on the values and the culture of computer professionals.

Hofstede defined culture as *"The collective programming of the mind which distinguishes the members of one group or category of people from another"*.[56] He classified what were originally four value dimensions of culture against which his research showed that certain countries differed.[57] Initially, he plotted forty nationalities against those four dimensions.[58] After further research, he extended his dimensions to five and plotted data from fifty countries and three regions against those five dimensions. The five dimensions are outlined as follows:

1. Power distance.
2. Uncertainty avoidance.
3. Individualism versus collectivism.
4. Masculinity versus femininity.
5. Long-term versus short-term orientation.

The *power distance* dimension relates to how people react to inequality and how they accept the unequal distribution of power within their society or organisation. This acceptance manifests itself in the way it impacts on

---

[54] Hofstede, G., Cultures and organizations: software of the mind 1991, London, UK: McGraw-Hill.
Hofstede, G., Culture's Consequences: Comparing Values, Behaviours, Institutions and Organizations Across Nations. 2001, Thousand Oaks, USA: Sage Publications.

[55] Hofstede, G., Culture's Consequences: Comparing Values, Behaviours, Institutions and Organizations Across Nations. 2001, Thousand Oaks, USA: Sage Publications.

[56] Hofstede, G., Cultures and organizations: software of the mind 1991, London, UK: McGraw-Hill.

[57] Schneider, S.C. and J.-L. Barsoux, Managing Across Cultures 2nd ed. 2002, Harlow: Financial Times Prentice Hall.

[58] Crow, G. and B. Muthuswamy, International Outsourcing in the Information Technology Industry: Trends and Implications. Communications of the International Information Management Association, 2003 3(1): p. 25 - 34.

relationships between managers, colleagues and subordinates.[59] How particular cultures respect hierarchy is demonstrated by how individuals behave toward those in authority and how they express themselves as a result.

Hofstede has defined *uncertainty avoidance* as the mechanism which different cultures employ to cope with the uncertainty of life. Societies have devised three strategies to address the issue of uncertainty: they are technology, law and religion. These mechanisms are established in accordance with the historical heritage, values and norms of the society – on which they are based - and are transferred and reinforced through the socialising instruments of the family, education and the state.

The term "technology" in this context is used in the broad sense i.e. that which includes all human artefacts. The development and implementation of technology provides predictability in an uncertain and ever changing world. Laws are the rules that guide social behaviour and facilitate the orderly operation of society. In the organisational context, rules are the mechanism utilised to address the uncertainty of its members' behaviour. Religion provides a mechanism for addressing the unknown and rituals allow us to communicate with a higher power in this setting. Religion and rituals are also a cohesive mechanism for binding a group together. Within the organisational setting, there is a need for social cohesion and the limitation of uncertainty. Rituals help to address both of these issues.

Different nationalities react to uncertainty in different ways and the structures and beliefs they have developed to address such issues are dependent on their specific culture. Hofstede points out that "*uncertainty avoidance is not the same as risk avoidance*".[60] He states that uncertainty is to risk what anxiety is to fear; the difference being that risk is focused on an event while fear is focused on an object. Anxiety has no object attached to it. Risk can be calculated as a probability percentage, whereas uncertainty has no probability that can be ascribed to it. In the case of uncertainty, anything can happen. In this context, certain cultures endeavour to avoid ambiguity. In contrast, cultures with low uncertainty avoidance prefer less structure, fewer written rules, and are more willing to take risks.

---

[59] Schneider, S.C. and J.-L. Barsoux, Managing Across Cultures 2nd ed. 2002, Harlow: Financial Times Prentice Hall.

[60] Hofstede, G., Cultures and organizations: software of the mind 1991, London, UK: McGraw-Hill.

Hofstede's third cultural dimension is *individualism versus collectivism* and it describes the relationship of the individual to groups within their society. The collectivist's preference is to be part of a closely-knit community which provides mutual care and support. The individualist's penchant is to be part of a more loosely-knit society. Cultures with a collectivist value system see the needs of the group (i.e. the organisation) and its welfare as more important then the individuals' needs. The maintenance of harmony within the family, the organisation and the society generally is considered a virtue and confrontation is therefore avoided. The word 'no' is not used very frequently, as saying no is considered confrontational. Similarly, the word 'yes' does not necessarily indicate approval. In contrast, individualists see their own needs as paramount and this is reflected in their approach to work and their attitude to membership of an organisation. The individualist's objective is self-advancement and while the goals of the organisation tie in with this, the individualist will support it.

The fourth cultural dimension is *masculinity versus femininity*. Masculine values are described as *"ego goals"* such as career and money. In the organisational setting, Hofstede has outlined the following as being more important for men: advancement, earning, training and up-to-dateness.[61] He defined feminine values as being "*social goal*" centric. Importance is placed on relationships, helping others and the physical environment. Within the organisation, the important values for women are outlined as a friendly atmosphere, position security, physical conditions and cooperation.

At the societal level, different nationalities demonstrate a predominance for masculine or feminine values. In masculine societies, competitive traits including success, assertiveness and performance are valued. This is in contrast to more feminine focused societies which value relationships, quality of life, and caring for others. At the organisational level, when individuals from masculine and feminine value-based societies work together, the difference in focus and approach can sometimes lead to misunderstandings. Behaviour, which in one culture is considered acceptable, can be offensive and unacceptable to individuals from the other. This can also lead to a divergence in the overall goals and objectives

[61] Hofstede, G., Cultures and organizations: software of the mind 1991, London, UK: McGraw-Hill.

of both groups and impact on the level of motivation and trust between culturally diverse colleagues.

Hofstede's fifth and final dimension is *long-term versus short-term orientation.* This dimension was developed independently of the other four. It was derived from Hofstede's collaborative work with Michael Bond and from the analysis of answers to his Chinese Value Survey (CVS). Bond's results were compared with Hofstede's and a fifth dimension emerged.[62] The kernel of this issue here is the extent to which cultures are oriented toward a long-term outlook as compared with those whose focus is more short term.

Long-term orientation is identified by its objective of achieving long-term goals including perseverance, the ordering of relationships by status, thrift and a sense of common shame; while low importance is ascribed to leisure and traditions which are adaptable. Short-term orientation is identified by focusing on the past and present and by expecting quick results. Status is not a major issue in such relationships. Shame is not a common feeling. Spending is acceptable and expected. Leisure time is considered important and there is a respect for tradition.

### 1.5.2 Culture is Communication

A complimentary approach to that of Hofstede's in understanding culture in the virtual team setting, is the work of Edward T. Hall. In his view, culture is communication and communication can be separated into three elements - words, material things and behaviour. Words are the medium for verbal expression. Material things can be an expression of status, wealth and power. Behaviour is an expression of how an individual feels or reacts to a situation, people or event. Hall cites the example of the politician who makes a speech which is meant to reassure the public but whose manner of delivery ensures that it has the opposite effect. On paper the words are reassuring, but the delivery has a negative impact.[63] In Hall's view, the study of the constituent elements of communication can ensure an understanding of the unconsciously expressed or "*silent language*". A study of this *silent language* provides insight into the principles that shape individuals and cultures. Hall equates culture to a

---

[62] Hofstede, G. and M.H. Bond, The Confucius connection: From Cultural Roots To Economic Growth. Organizational Dynamics, 1988. 16(4): p. 5 - 21.
[63] Hall, E.T. The Silent Language. 1959, Westport, Connecticut, USA: Greenwood Press.

computer which has programs that guide human responses and reactions. Crucially, the cultural program will not work if important elements are missing. This happens when individuals unconsciously apply their own rules to another system. This concept is not dissimilar to Hofstede's view of culture as "*software of the mind*".[64]

Hall defined seven concepts, which he identified as relevant to the study of national and corporate culture:

1. Speed of messages.
2. Context.
3. Space.
4. Time.
5. Information flow.
6. Action chains.
7. Interfacing.

The *speed of messages* varies. A fast message can be the news headlines on the radio or television, a newspaper headline or a cartoon. A slow message takes longer to decipher. It can be a book, a piece of art or an in-depth study. Slow messages can only be understood by those who take the time to decipher them and who have the knowledge to determine their meaning. Speed of message has a specific relevance to the operation of virtual teams given the constraints in which they have to operate.

*Context* is the information around a particular communication, item or event. This information provides those additional elements which come together to give it its full meaning. This level of information or context can be described as either high or low.

> "A high-context communication or message is one in which the information is either in the physical context or is internalized in the person… A low context message is just the opposite i.e. the mass of the information is vested in the explicit code".[65]

Different cultures can be described as either high-context or low-context. In high context cultures extensive background information is not required. A lot of information can be transmitted by non-verbal signs which need to

---

[64] Hall, E.T. and M. Reed Hall, Understanding cultural differences. 1990, Yarmouth, Maine, USA: Intercultural Press, Inc.

[65] Hall, E.T., Beyond Culture Vol. Doubleday. 1981: Anchor Books.

be read and understood. In low context societies professional and personal relationships tend to be kept separate. In this situation, more background information needs to be provided. Communication needs to be clear and to the point. In these cultures people do not expect to have to read between the lines of what is being presented. In the virtual team environment, a large percentage of communication takes place in an asynchronous environment and there may be no opportunity for visual contact.

*Space* is important culturally and different cultures require different amounts of personal space. Space can also equate to power and position. In some cultures, if an individual has a large office, this is an indication of their power and status. In other cultures managers are happy to be located with their subordinates. In the virtual team setting - other than when an individual is meeting remote colleagues, visiting a remote site, or has responsibility for establishing infrastructure in that location - space is not a major area of concern. That said, this is a topic about which the Project Managers and Team Leaders should be aware.

Different cultures have different attitudes to *time*. Hall describes the two cultural approaches to time as monochronic and polychronic.[66] Monochronic time is linear in nature and segmented. Monochronic cultures carry out sequential activities. They plan extensively in order to maximise the available time and time commitments are taken very seriously. The job is more important than the individual. On the other hand, polychronic cultures are the opposite, since they carry out simultaneous activities and time commitments are considered flexible. Plans may change frequently and easily. There is an emphasis on human relationships rather than keeping to the schedule. These conflicting approaches to time and their potential impacts on the operation of virtual teams are considerable.

*Information flows* to different locations. In low context cultures, information is controlled and focused on those who need to know. In high-context cultures, information flows freely around the organisation. People are informed and make it their business to stay up-to-date on what is going on. The importance of information flow in the virtual team context is clear. Where low and high context team members are on the same virtual team, the effective mechanisms for managing information flow need to be considered and addressed.

---

[66] Hall, E.T., Beyond Culture Vol. Doubleday. 1981: Anchor Books.

*Action chains* are the ritual of doing business, where step one must be completed before step two is undertaken. Bureaucratic processes, software development, and test procedures are all based on the action-chain approach. The breaking of the action chain can, in certain circumstances, have serious repercussions. The importance of the action chain also needs to be taken into account when planning. Low-context, monochronic cultures experience great difficulty when the chain is broken, as they find it difficult to deal with unexpected change. High-context polychronic cultures find change easier to deal with. Opposing views for ensuring change to the action chain have the potential to lead to conflict. In the virtual team situation, it is important that there is an awareness of the different cultural approaches to change and how they can impact on the action chain.

The concept of effective *interfacing* is a key element in the business environment when dealing with cultural diversity and has specific relevance for virtual team environments. An effective interfacer is an individual who is a bridge between team members, departments, organisations and cultures. These individuals need to have a knowledge of the cultures they are interfacing between. They are a bridgehead between locations and are an effective point of contact for local and remote staff who seek and transmit information to one another.

### 1.5.3 The Layered Nature of Culture

Trompenaars and Hampden-Turner (1998) equate culture to an onion that comes in layers and has to be peeled in order to be understood. They have developed seven dimensions of culture. Each of these seven dimensions provides a juxtapositional view of the different aspects of culture, including:

1. Universalism versus particularism.
2. Individualism versus communitarianism.
3. '*Specific*' versus diffuse.
4. Affective versus neutral.
5. Achievement versus ascription.
6. Sequential versus synchronic.
7. Internal versus external control.

*Universalism versus particularism* outlines two cultural approaches to what is considered good and correct. In the cultural setting, universalism implies that there is a set of defined rules which are correct and which should be implemented in all circumstances. This is contrasted with particularism which places a special value or emphasis on relationships and circumstances rather then on rules.

*Individualism versus communitarianism* is similar in approach to Hofstede's individualism versus collectivism dimension.[67]

*'Specific' versus diffuse cultures*: In a '*specific*' culture, business and home are separate and compartmentalised. Individuals from a '*specific*' culture concentrate on hard facts, standards and contracts. They can be described as direct, open and extrovert. Diffuse cultures are the opposite, however i.e. - there is a large "personal" side to people's lives. This is reflected in their business relationships and they are often considered to be introverted, closed and indirect.

*Affective versus neutral*: These terms are used to describe the acceptability of showing emotion. In affective cultures, people show their feelings and it is an acceptable practice. In a neutral culture it is the opposite; the expression of feelings is controlled and individuals are not encouraged to display their feelings publicly.

*Achievement versus ascription*: In an achievement-based culture, status is gained from what the individual has and is capable of achieving. In an ascribed culture, status is derived from who someone is and what position or role they hold.

*Sequential versus synchronic* cultures relates to time and the ordering of tasks. The sequential approach is to see time as a narrow band and plan accordingly. Therefore, the achievement of milestones and deadlines is very important. Synchronic cultures, on the other hand, see time as a wide ribbon. In this situation, multi-tasking is acceptable - time and deadlines are considered flexible and plans can be easily changed. The similarities between monochronic and polychromic time, as outlined by Edward Hall, are clear.

---

[67] Hofstede, G., Riding the Waves of Commerce: A test of Trompenaars' 'Model'of National Cultural Differences. International Journal of Intercultural Relations 1996. 20(2): p. 189-198.
Hampden-Turner, C. and F. Trompenaars, Response to Geert Hofstede. International Journal of Intercultural Relations, 1997. 21(1): p. 149-159.

*Internal versus external control.* Every culture has developed its own way of dealing with nature. Do individuals control nature or does nature control them? Cultures with an internalist viewpoint perceive the environment as mechanical and something that can be controlled. Their view is that an individual can achieve the life they desire if they take the opportunities which they are given. Externalists, on the other hand, view themselves and their environment as a part of nature. They have to go along with what happens and they believe they have very little control over their own destiny.

## 1.6 The Research Focus

Having undertaken an extensive literature review, it was clear that considerable research has previously been carried out in the general area of GSD. It was equally evident that there was room for additional research to be undertaken on this subject. This was confirmed by the recent (and increased) level of interest in the area from the software industry as a whole and by the number of requests and offers of support for such research emerging from organisations employing a GSD-based strategy. As a result of undertaking the literature review, a number of areas emerged which provided a specific and unique focus for this research.

The literature highlighted a number of problems with GSD and the operation of virtual teams. These issues included communication, distance (cultural, temporal and geographical), and project management. However, it was clear that additional research could confirm and expand the level of knowledge of these areas. There was also the possibility of identifying additional or supplementary factors that had not previously been recognised.

In addition, at the macro level, an important problem was the need for the development of a specific GSD-centric process.[68] It is recognised that GSD has a profound impact on the way in which products are conceived, designed, constructed and tested.[69] To be effective, this process needs to

---

[68] Kiyaev, V., et al. Formalization and Automation of Global Software Development Processes. in The 2nd International Workshop New Models of Business. Managerial Aspects and Enabling Technology. 2002. St. Petersburg.

[69] Prikladnicki, R., J.L.N. Audy, and R. Evaristo. An Empirical Study on Global Software Development: Offshore Insourcing of IT Projects. in The International Workshop on Global Software Development, International Conference on Software Engineering (ICSE 2004). 2004. Edinburgh, Scotland: IEEE.

be generic in nature and should efficiently address and leverage the key variables and infrastructure, which facilitate effective GSD. At the micro level, one of the key areas within such a process is the establishment and operation of software testing teams. The literature review indicated that relatively little research had been carried out in the specific area of the operation of globally distributed software testing teams.

### 1.6.1 Software Testing

Effective software testing plays a key role in delivering high quality products.[70] Testing is a labour intensive and expensive activity which can equate to half the total cost of some software projects.[71] However, testing has not received the attention its importance clearly merits. *"Software testing is arguably the least understood part of the development process".*[72] In fact, software testing has been described as the '*Cinderella*' of software development.[73] Although the number of books and papers published on this topic has increased over the last number of years, "*less seems to be known about software testing than about any other aspect of software development…testing remains among the 'dark arts*'".

This being the situation for collocated software testing teams, it was not surprising to find that the situation for globally distributed testing was similar. To date, very little work has been done which has focused on the specific area of GSD testing. Where the subject was discussed, it was generally in terms of "*development teams in emerging countries are willing to do the unglamorous tasks such as…testing*".[74]

---

[70] Pressman, R.S. and D. Adapted by Ince, Software Engineering: A Practitioner's Approach. Fourth ed. 1997, New York: McGraw-Hill Companies Inc. 885.

[71] Endres, A. and D. Rombach, A Handbook of Software and Systems Engineering: Empirical Observations, Laws and Theories. 2003, Harlow, UK: Pearson Addison Wesley. 327.

Myers, G.J., et al., The Art of Software Testing. Second ed. 2004, New Jersey, U.S.A: John Wiley and Sons. 234.

[72] Whitaker, J.A., What Is Software Testing? And Why Is It So Hard. IEEE Software, 2000. 17(1): p. 70 - 79.

[73] Ince, D.C., Has Testing Practice Improved Over The Last Twenty Years? IEE Colloquium on Software Testing for Critical Systems, 1990: p. 1/1 -1/2.

[74] Carmel, E. Thirteen Assertions for Globally Dispersed Software Development Research. in 30th Hawaii International Conference on System Sciences (HICSS) 1997. Hawaii.

GSD testing was perceived as a "*less attractive and better defined task*"[75]that lent itself to being outsourced or offshored. It was also considered a solitary activity[76] one which also made it suitable for GSD. In these terms, testing was perceived as a relatively straightforward activity that was not negatively impacted upon by issues such as communication, culture and coordination.[77] While this view was put forward in the literature, little detailed evidence to support the totality of this perspective was evident. Having identified this gap, this study focused on testing.

### 1.6.2 Virtual Teams Operation

The next step was to determine the most appropriate method of globally distributed development testing to investigate. Having reviewed the alternatives, was determined that the study of virtual software testing would be the most beneficial, given that the nature of this type of operation exposes the virtual team members to the full impact of operating in a globally distributed environment.

#### 1.6.2.1 The Virtual Team in Context

Given that the focus of this work is the operation of virtual teams, there is a need to set the term "virtual team" in context. The virtual team has been described as the core building block of the virtual organisation.[78] What are the characteristics of a virtual team? A traditional team is defined as a social group of individuals who are collocated and interdependent in their tasks. The group undertakes and coordinates their activities to achieve

---

[75] Edwards, H.K. and V. Sridhar. Analysis of the effectiveness of global virtual teams in software engineering projects. in The 36th Hawaii International Conference on System Sciences. 2003. Hawaii.
[76] Sahay, S., B. Nicholson, and S. Krishna, Global IT Outsourcing: Software Development across Borders. 2003, Cambridge UK: Cambridge University Press.
[77] McGregor, D., The Human Side of Enterprise 1960 New York, Toronto, London.: McGraw-Hill Book Company, Inc.
[78] Jarvenpaa, S.L. and B. Ives, The Global Network Organization of the Future: Information Management Opportunities and Challenges,. Journal of Management Science and Information Systems, 1994. 10(4): p. 25 - 57.
Mohrman, S., Albers, The Context for Geographically Dispersed Teams and Networks. The Virtual Organization (Trends in Organizational Behaviour), ed. C.L. Cooper and D.M. Rousseau. Vol. 6. 1999, Chichester: John Wiley & Sons. 63 - 80.

common goals and shares the responsibility for outcomes.[79] Virtual teams have the same goals and objectives as traditional teams and interact through interdependent tasks, but they tend to operate across time, geographical location and organisational boundaries linked by communication technologies. They normally operate in a multicultural and multilingual environment which may traverse organisational boundaries.[80]

Communication between virtual team members is normally electronic and asynchronous with limited opportunities for synchronous contact, depending on time zones. The team may function on a permanent or a temporary basis which is contingent on the demands of the business environment within which it is operating.

Organisations in many different sectors of the economy implement a virtual team strategy. The focus of this research is on the operation of virtual teams in the software development environment and with specific reference to those undertaking the testing process. When the term virtual software testing team is utilised in this monograph, it refers to: *A team made up of members situated in more than one location who are geographically, culturally and temporally distant and operate across divisional lines, while being interdependent in their testing tasks.* Their overall objective is to function as a single team who have the same goals as if they were in a collocated situation and in which they can successfully undertake software product testing.

### 1.6.2.2 The Rationale for Selecting a Virtual Team Strategy

The rationale organisations have for implementing a virtual team based software development strategy are varied. An important factor which has been recognised is that GSD is not without its inherent business-related

---

[79] Powell, A., G. Piccoli, and B. Ives, Virtual Teams: A Review of Current Literature and Direction for Future Research. The DATA BASE for Advances in Information Systems, 2004. 35(1): p. 6 - 36.

[80] DeSanctis, G., N. Staudenmayer, and S.S. Wong, Interdependence in Virtual Organizations. The Virtual Organization (Trends in Organizational Behaviour), ed. C.L. Cooper and D.M. Rousseau. Vol. 6. 1999, Chichester: John Wiley and Sons. 81 - 104.

risks.[81] This has a particular relevance when organisational boundaries are crossed. There can be aspects of a software application which provide competitive advantage to the organisation that are having it developed.[82] Therefore, they may not wish to grant access to such information to an outside organisation, even if they are temporarily partnered with them. In this situation, the implementation of a virtual team strategy is one method that can be employed to allow the equal division of the development across various sites. The activities that need to remain confidential are undertaken by the organisation's own virtual team members whereas related activities are undertaken by external remote team colleagues.

Another appropriate circumstance for utilising a virtual team strategy can be when software development is carried out exclusively outside the offshoring or outsourcing location. The capability to maintain and to develop the software further can be lost to those who have outsourced the work. To address this problem, virtual teams may be utilised to ensure that core knowledge and competency are maintained within the division or organisation.

The implementation of a virtual team strategy can also be a simple cost-based decision. This can be achieved by combining the technical skills and experience of staff located in a high-cost centre with those of a group of engineers in a low-cost location. This may be implemented as a long-term or short-term approach, depending on the overall objectives of the organisation. If the goal is a short-term strategy, then it may simply be used as a knowledge-transfer exercise. If, on the other hand, it is a long-term objective, sustained support will be required for team member at all locations.

### 1.6.3 Distributed Teams versus Virtual Teams

There is a level of ambiguity in the literature regarding the use of the two terms *distributed team* and *virtual team*. Many authors on the subject have

---

[81] Herbsleb, J.D., et al. Distance, Dependencies and Delay in Global Collaboration. in Proceedings of the 2000 ACM conference on Computer supported cooperative work 2000. Philadelphia, Pennsylvania, USA ACM Press.

[82] Herbsleb, J.D., et al. Distance, Dependencies and Delay in Global Collaboration. in Proceedings of the 2000 ACM conference on Computer supported cooperative work 2000. Philadelphia, Pennsylvania, USA ACM Press.

used the terms interchangeably[83] *"'Geographically distributed team' is another descriptive name for what many people now call a 'virtual team'"*.[84] While it is now common practice to use both terms for describing the same thing – in the context of this volume - it is important to highlight the difference. To achieve this objective, we look to the work of Lipnack and Stamp (1997) both of whom are widely quoted for defining the term virtual team.[85]

*"Distributed teams comprise people in the same organization who work in different places. They may operate interdependently"*[86]or they may not. The term distributed team simply states the geographical location of the team members in the same organisation. The important difference between a virtual team and a distributed team can be considered as the interdependence of the various tasks. A key element of any virtual team is the interdependence of tasks. This is not necessarily the case for all distributed teams, however.

In this context, it can be said that all virtual teams are distributed ones, but not all distributed teams have to be virtual. It is possible to have a team which is geographically distributed but where the work has been divided out in such a manner that there is no interdependence of tasks between team members. In these circumstances, this team is distributed but not virtual. The teams researched in this monograph were distributed virtual teams where there was a clear interdependence of tasks between team members at both locations.

---

[83] Dafoulas, G. and M. Linda, Investigating Cultural Differences in Virtual Software Teams. The Electronic Journal on Information Systems in Developing Countries 2001. 7(4): p. 1 -14.

[84] Anschuetz, L. Managing geographically distributed teams. in IPPC 98 Proceedings the annual conference of the IEEE Professional Communication Society. 1998.

[85] Maznevski, M.L. and K.M. Chudoba, Bridging Space Over Time: Global Virtual Team Dynamics and Effectiveness. Organization Science, 2000. 11(5): p. 473–492.

Sarker, S. and S. Sahay, Understanding virtual team development: An interpretive study. Journal of the Association for Information Systems, 2002. 3: p. 247-285.

Wong, S.-S. and R.M. Burton, Virtual teams: what are their characteristics and impact on team performance? Computational and Mathematical Organization Theory, 2001. 6(4): p. 339 - 60.

[86] Boehm, B.W. and R. Ross, Theory-W Software Project Management Principles And Examples. IEEE Transactions on Engineering Management, 1989. 15(7): p. 902 – 916.

## 1.7 The Research Problem Defined

The initial objective of this research was to study the operations of management and staff who have previously been offshored or outsourced to – and who are now responsible for offshoring their own work. This was facilitated by the research taking place in Ireland. The second objective was to focus on the operation of software testing teams. The third and final objective was to undertake this research within an organisation that was implementing a virtual software testing team strategy. Having determined the research focus, the research problem was defined as follows:

> The identification of the key factors, infrastructure, methods, process and procedures, which facilitate and hinder effective globally distributed software virtual team testing.

The interest and support of Computing World (Ireland) Ltd. in the subject of this research and their willingness to participate by granting access to their organisation ensured that this investigation could be undertaken.

## 1.8 The Semantics of Offshoring and Outsourcing

Given that the evolution of the virtual team and GSD is a phenomenon of the 1990s, it is not surprising that the vocabulary associated with these operations is still currently being defined. This is clearly illustrated by the use of the terms *outsourcing* and *offshoring*. When organisations embark on a geographically-distributed software development strategy, are they outsourcing or offshoring?

The answer to this question is that there is no definitive delineation of the term offshoring.[87] The term offshoring has been used to describe a number of business endeavours including foreign investment activities.[88]

---

[87] Schultze, C., Offshoring, Import Competition, and the Jobless Recovery. The Brookings Institution Policy Brief, 2004(136): p. 1 - 8.
Government, International Trade: Current Government Data Provide Limited insight into Offshoring Services, U.S.G.A. Office, Editor. 2004, Accountability Office United States Government p. 1 - 54.
Chakraborty, K. and W. Remington, "Offshoring" of IT services: the impact on the US economy Journal of Computing Sciences in Colleges 2005 20(4), p. 112-125.

[88] Chakraborty, K. and W. Remington, "Offshoring" of IT services: the impact on the US economy Journal of Computing Sciences in Colleges 2005 20(4), p. 112-125.

Offshore sourcing has been defined as including "*both offshore outsourcing to a third party as well as offshore insourcing within the global corporation*".[89]

The Government of the United States[90] defines offshoring in terms of a business or a Government decision to source a service from an offshore location rather then producing it internally or sourcing it domestically. It goes on to state that a less frequent use of the term describes investment by organisations in offshore operations, with the objective of transferring all or part of their production offshore. This latter definition has become familiar to the general public due to its prolific use in the media particularly in the USA where GSD has received considerable public attention and debate.[91] The term offshoring can be further characterised in its popular sense i.e. to describe companies relocating part of what was their domestic operation to affiliates, which they own and control, and which are based in foreign locations.

Outsourcing can be defined as the transfer of production or the sourcing of a service to an independent and external organisation, be this domestically or internationally located.[92] While this definition is generally accepted within the software industry, the term outsourcing has been used to describe the situation where an organisation sets up an affiliate in a foreign location and transfers production there. This was the situation in the organisation where this research was undertaken.

In 1999, the Computing World Corporation set up the Computing World (Far Eastern Software Centre). In 2004, Computing World (Ireland) Ltd. was in the process of transferring part of its testing function to an Asian country, through the use of a virtual team strategy. This activity could be

---

[89] Carmel, E. and R. Agarwal, The Maturation of Offshore Sourcing of Information Technology Work. MIS Quarterly Executive 2002. 1(2): p. 65 -77.

[90] Government, International Trade: Current Government Data Provide Limited insight into Offshoring Services, U.S.G.A. Office, Editor. 2004, Accountability Office United States Government p. 1 - 54.

[91] Thottam, J., Is Your Job Going Abroad?, in Time Magazine. 2004.
McLaughlin, L. An Eye On India: Outsourcing Debate Continues. IEEE Software, 2003. 20(3): p. 114- 117.
Levy, D.L., Offshoring in the New Global Political Economy. Journal of Management Studies 2005, 42(3): p. 685 - 693.

[92] Levy, D.L., Offshoring in the New Global Political Economy. Journal of Management Studies 2005, 42(3): p. 685 - 693.

considered offshoring according to the popular definition of that term. Within this organisation, activities which related to this work were consistently referred to as outsourcing. For the purposes of this volume, and in the interests of clarity, what the members of this organisation referred to as outsourcing has been described as offshoring. The only exception to this rule is where direct quotes are used.

## 1.9 Structure of This Volume

This chapter has introduced the scope of the research area, the literature review and have placed both in context. Globalisation and the operation of virtual teams has been discussed and virtual software testing has been identified as the focus for this analysis. Based on this focus, the research problem has been outlined in more depth and the rationale for its selection articulated.

In chapter two, the research approach is discussed and the data collection strategy is outlined. Consideration is given to the analysis of the data and the selection of a qualitative approach is described. The reasons for the selection of a Yin-based case study, action research and the utilisation of a grounded theory strategy are all outlined. These various approaches are all considered at length and the reasons for their selection discussed in light of the available literature and requirements of this research investigation.

Chapter three presents an overview of the organisation where the on-site aspects of this research were undertaken. The teams which provided the focus for this research and the organisation's offshoring strategy are also presented. The practicality of the initial participant observational research which included an extensive on-site document review is also considered.

The focus of chapter four is the building of concepts and categories based on the gathered data. This includes microanalysis, a process which encompassed the utilisation of open coding, axial coding and memo writing. This, in turn, facilitated the identification of the initial concepts which provided the basis for the identification of categories. These categories were further analysed utilising selective coding and led to the classification of three high-level categories in addition to a central category

The question of culture is explored in chapter five. A lack of understanding for the culture of remote virtual members and the operation of the virtual teams is discussed. Specific issues which were identified here include gender, religion, power-distance and the implication of remote colleagues saying "yes" to every request. The impact which fear has on the day-to-day operation of virtual teams as a result of cultural difference is also explored.

In chapter six, communication in the virtual team setting is considered. The importance of opportunities for virtual team members to communicate with one another is explored through a discussion on language and the ability to communicate effectively. The availability of effective communication tools and the desire to utilise them in order to facilitate communication is also considered. The need for a well-defined common vocabulary and a clearly-documented communication procedure is discussed. Fear and the impact it has in hindering effective communication taking place is also explored.

The focus of chapter seven is on project management in the virtual software testing team environment. The nature of GSD and its impact on effective project management is discussed. The specific areas that are addressed here include the evaluation of risk and true cost, the need for a documented process and the provision of adequate infrastructure to support the operation of virtual teams. The selection, organisation and operation of teams is considered at length and a particular emphasis is placed on the need for team building and cooperation, particularly given the impact which fear can have on the management of virtual teams.

Chapter eight addresses the impact which fear has on virtual team operation. The basis for the level of fear identified by this research is outlined and its implications for the day-to-day operation of virtual teams is also discussed. Fear has a particularly negative impact on motivation and trust levels and on the operation of the teams as a whole. It also proved a major problem which negatively impacted on the various other high-level categories which this investigation identified.

Chapter nine outlines the key factors and conclusions drawn from this investigation and places them in context, while also providing specific answers to the research questions. It also identifies the research contribution made by this particular study. Finally, opportunities for further research as based on this work are considered in some detail.

# CHAPTER TWO

# RESEARCH METHODS AND IMPLEMENTATION

## 2. Research Approach

The overall strategy adopted for this research was to build theory through the identification and selection of the most appropriate research paradigm, methodology and strategy. The objective of this chapter is to outline the approach taken to this research project based on the requirements, constraints and objectives of this investigation.

## 2.1 Research Paradigms

A theory is defined as a statement concerning the relationships between the different variables or concepts and as a network of hypotheses put forward to conceptualise and explain particular social or natural phenomena.[1] A hypothesis presents an assertion about the relationship between two or more concepts. Concepts are defined as the building blocks of theory and hypothesis. They are the abstract ideas which are used to classify elements sharing common properties.[2] Theories also shape how people explain what it is that they observe.[3] In social science research there are two distinct strategies employed for the development and validation of theory – i.e. the deductive and inductive methods. Both strategies have the same objective and the primary difference between both is the approach taken and the particular methods employed.

---

[1] Ezzy, D., Qualitative Analysis Practice and Innovation. 2002, London UK: Routledge.

[2] Gill, J. and P. Johnson, Research Methods for Managers, ed. Second. 1997, London UK.

[3] Ezzy, D., Qualitative Analysis Practice and Innovation. 2002, London UK: Routledge.

### 2.1.1 Deductive Theory Building

The deductive theory-building approach is defined as the development of a conceptual and theoretical view prior to the testing of hypotheses. Testing is then carried out on the hypotheses. Data generated is then analysed and used to confirm or reject these hypotheses. The deductive strategy is positivist in its approach as its methodology is derived from the traditional scientific procedures for undertaking research.[4]

The component elements of the deductive approach are defined as in (Figure 2.1). Concepts which represent key aspects of the area under investigation are identified and these concepts are used to formulate theories and hypotheses. Rules are developed to determine when an instance of the concept has occurred, thereby ensuring that it is observational in approach. This operationalised approach takes an abstract concept and defines the indicators which are measurable. By standardising results, a reliable measure of the concepts under investigation can be derived. An important aspect of these indicators is that they are publicly observable and can therefore be repeated and calibrated. Empirical data is collected and compared with the indicators to determine the validity of the theories and hypotheses. Based on these results, theories and hypotheses are either corroborated or rejected.

### 2.1.2 Inductive Theory Building

The inductive theory building approach is the opposite of the deductive strategy. In inductive theory, observation of the empirical world is utilised as the basis for developing concepts and theories. The inductive approach can be illustrated by the grounded theory research method which was developed in part as a reaction to the more deductive methods. The essence of the inductive approach and the grounded theory approach is that it is "*grounded*" in data observation and comparison. In this approach, observation is not based on any pre-conceived theories. Instead, it is the observation and analysis of data which leads to the development of theories.[5] The simple inductive theory building strategy outlined in Figure 2.2 illustrates the key components of the inductive grounded theory

---

[4] Bryman, A., Quantity and Quality in Social Research Contemporary Social Research, ed. M. Blumer. Vol. 18. 1988, London: Routledge.

[5] Glaser, B. and A. Strauss, The Discovery of Grounded Theory: strategies for qualitative research ,. 1967, New York: Aldine de Gruyter.

approach. Research is undertaken here without the goal of validating any preconceived theories.[6]

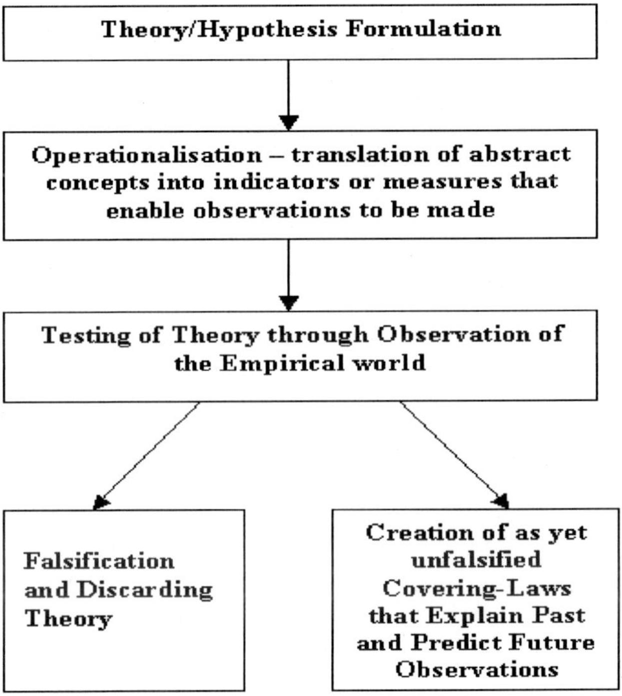


Figure 2.1: Deductive Theory Building

This method is rooted in the systematic gathering of data, data which is then observed and analysed. This analysis and observation is structured by the sampling which also facilitates constant comparison. Based on this analysis and comparison, various inferences can be drawn and used as the basis for developing theory.[7] It is assumed that, as the theories emerge

---

6 Strauss, A. and J. Corbin, Basics of Qualitative Research: Techniques and Procedures for Developing Grounded Theory. Second ed. 1998, Thousand Oaks, CA, USA: Sage Publications.

7 Gomm, R., Social Research Methodology: A Critical Introduction. 2004, Basingstoke Palgrave Macmillan.

Creswell, J.W., Research design : qualitative and quantitative approaches 1994, Thousand Oaks, CA, USA: Sage Publications.

from the data, they are more reflective of reality than those derived from a more positivist approach.[8] It has been argued that the simplistic inductive grounded theory method offers advantages over the deductive approach.[9] That view is not without its critics however, and the ability to carry out research in a truly theory-neutral manner is considered difficult, if not impossible. While the limitations of the inductive approach are acknowledged, the proponents of this research method believe it is better to commence research with an open mind rather than with the objective of testing pre-formulated hypotheses.[10]

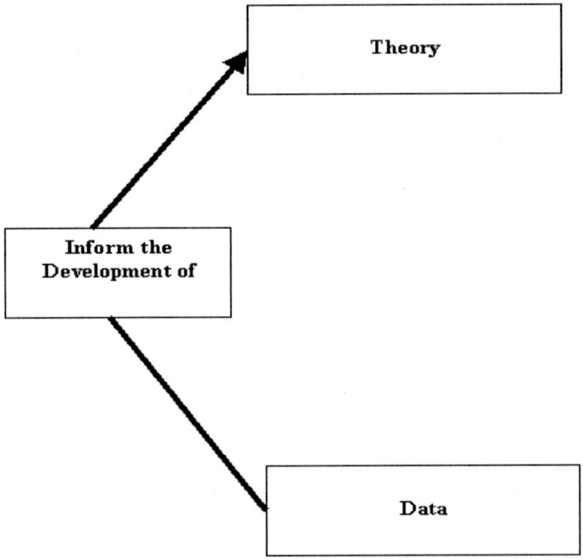


Figure 2.2: Simplistic Inductive Theory Building

[8] Strauss, A. and J. Corbin, Basics of Qualitative Research : Techniques and Procedures for Developing Grounded Theory. Second ed. 1998, Thousand Oaks, CA, USA: Sage Publications.
[9] Glaser, B.G., The Basics of Grounded Theory Analysis : Emergence vs Forcing. 1992, Mill Valley, CA. USA: Sociology Press.
[10] Gomm, R., Social Research Methodology: A Critical Introduction. 2004, Basingstoke Palgrave Macmillan.

## 2.2 Quantitative and Qualitative Research Paradigms

A paradigm is defined as a cluster of beliefs or dictates which determine what should be studied, how that study should be undertaken, and how the results should be interpreted. It provides a framework in which effective research can be carried out. The difference in methodological assumptions between the qualitative and positivist, quantitative paradigms have been illustrated in the following ways. The positivist approach uses the quantitative and experimental methods of deductive hypothesis-testing. This is in contrast to the use of qualitative approaches which endeavour to understand human experience within its actual contexts and settings.[11]

### 2.2.1 Quantitative Research

Quantitative research is positivist in its approach. Its methods and philosophy are based on those employed in the natural sciences. It has a deductive structure where theories are formed as based on the subject areas being researched. Based on these theories, particular hypotheses are derived. These hypotheses are focused on causal relationships or concepts which can be quantifiably collaborated.

Data is observed, collated and numerically analysed. The results generated are then to corroborate or reject these hypotheses. The findings are then re-integrated so as to amend or confirm the original theories[12] (see Figure 2.3).

### 2.2.2 Qualitative Research

Qualitative research has been defined as

> "multi-method in focus, involving an interpretive, naturalistic approach to its subject matter. This means that qualitative researchers study things in their natural settings, attempting to make sense of, or interpret, phenomena in terms of the meanings people bring to them".[13]

---

[11] Patton Quinn, M., Qualitative Evaluation and Research Methods Second ed. 1990, London: Sage.

[12] Creswell, J.W., Research Design : qualitative and quantitative approaches 1994, Thousand Oaks, CA, USA: Sage Publications.

[13] Denzin, N.K. and Y.S. Lincoln, Handbook of Qualitative Research. 1984, Newbury Park: Sage Publications.

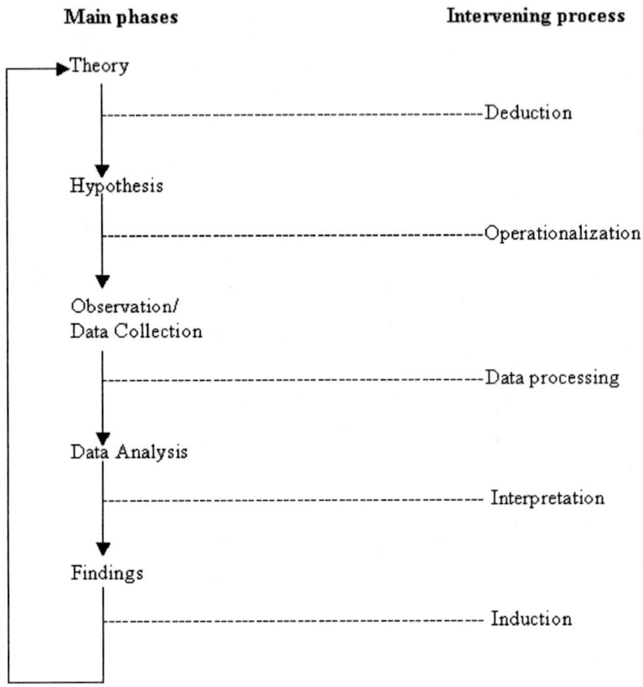


Figure 2.3: The Logical Structure of Quantitative Research

The focus of this approach is on getting inside particular working environments situations and viewing events, actions and norms from the perspective of the people being studied. Qualitative data is focused on naturally-occurring or ordinary events in natural settings which are grounded locally so as to reflect real-life situations. The research takes place within bounded cases as embedded in particular contexts. Data gathering methods employed include participant observation, interviews and document review. The qualitative data generated is subsequently analysed. This analysis may take the form of data reduction, data display, conclusion drawing or verification.[14] The results derived from this analysis are utilised in the development and verification of theories.

[14] Miles, M.B. and M.A. Huberman, Qualitative Data Analysis: An Expanded Sourcebook Second ed. 1994, London: Sage Publications.

### 2.2.3 Comparison between Paradigms

To appreciate the differences between the quantitative and the qualitative paradigms, they have been contrasted on five dimensions.[15] These dimensions compare the different approaches and philosophies underlying both paradigms:

- Ontology: The study of the nature of existence and reality.
- Epistemology: The study of the criteria for what does and does not constitute valid knowledge.
- Axiology: The study of values.
- Rhetoric: The use of language.
- Methodology: The methods by which the research is carried out and validated.

Applying this five-dimensional approach is an effective method for comparing and contrasting both the qualitative and quantitative paradigms. It is illustrative in nature however, and a practical implementation of either paradigm rarely contains all of the characteristics as outlined.

### 2.2.4 The Selection of the Research Paradigm

The selection of an applicable paradigm for this research was based on a direct comparison between each of the five dimensions outlined in (Creswell, 1994). The initial task was to make a comparison based on the *ontological* dimension. This research was based on virtual team interaction and operation. In these circumstances, reality could not be defined as objective and independent. The different views of reality as provided by those were researched needed to be reported, compared and analysed, all of which was consistent with the qualitative approach

The quantitative view of the *epistemological* dimension is that the researchers should remain independent from what they are researching. In this research it was important to maintain a participant observational position, one which allowed the establishment of one-to-one contact and facilitated the development of trust between the researcher and the subjects researched. In these circumstances, the qualitative approach was considered the most suitable.

---

[15] Creswell, J.W., Research Design : qualitative and quantitative approaches 1994, Thousand Oaks, CA, USA: Sage Publications.

When addressing the *axiological* dimension of this research, the quantitative view that values are kept out of research and that research should be based solely on "facts" was not considered a realistic approach. What any individual has determined as '*fact*' is based to some extent on some element of subjective bias and is influenced by the values of the person who has identified it. The qualitative approach was therefore considered a more realistic approach for this research.

Considering the use of *rhetoric*, the qualitative view is that the language used in reporting research should be informal and based on the concepts and definitions developed over the period of the study. Given the focus on human interaction in this research, this approach was considered the most appropriate.

When addressing the *methodological* dimension, the positivist approach of prior theory formulation and measured hypothesis validation was not considered applicable. As a consequence of these various comparisons, the qualitative research paradigm was selected as the most appropriate for carrying out this research. It was decided that an overall inductive approach should be undertaken for this research. While applying Creswell's criteria it is important to state that qualitative research does not have to be (simply) inductive in approach. Qualitative research can be considered positivist, interpretive or critical[16] depending on the researchers' philosophical assumptions.[17]

## 2.3 Selection of Research Methodology

There are three major components of qualitative research:

- Gathering Data - which can come from a number of sources - interviews, observation and documents.
- Analysis of Data (Coding) – reduction, display, conclusion drawing, verification.
- Writing up the Findings.

Methods of carrying out qualitative research include:

---

[16] Chua, W.F., Radical Developments in Accounting Thought. The Accounting Review, 1986. 61(4): p. 601-632.

[17] Klein, H.K. and M.D. Myers, A Set of Principles for Conducting and Evaluating Interpretive Field Studies in Information Systems. MIS Quarterly 1999. 23(1): p. pp. 67-93.

- An ethnographic study where the researcher studies a specific group of individuals in their cultural and natural location over a specified period of time.
- Grounded theory - which is inductive in its approach and facilitates the development of theories based on the analysis and comparison of data.
- A case study where the researcher studies a specific bounded case or a number of cases in a particular setting. This approach is implemented where there is a need to recognise the importance context plays in relation to the subject being researched.[18]
- Action research, which is a variant of quasi-experimental research. It entails the analysis of the direct intervention by the researcher. The classical approach is the five-phased cyclical approach as defined by Susman and Evered (1978) and as outlined in Baskerville (1997, 1999).

To select the most appropriate method or methods for undertaking this research the initial task was to carefully consider the opportunities and constraints within which it was to be undertaken.

### 2.3.1 The Opportunity Provided by On-site Based Research

Due to the support provided by a large multinational organisation called Computing World (a pseudonym) for this investigation, the opportunity was available for research to be undertaken on-site and within their organisation. The details of how this research was to be carried out had to be defined and agreed with Computing World (Ireland) Ltd. Therefore, it was necessary to have a planned and formalised approach which addressed these various important issues.

The opportunity for on-site access facilitated the implementation of a participant observational research role. It was recognised that in undertaking this approach the researcher could not claim total objectivity. Bearing this in mind, the data collection and data analysis methods implemented allowed for an inductive strategy whereby the full benefits of this access could be realised.

---

[18] Yin, R.K., Case study research / design and methods Second ed. Applied Social Research Methods Vol. 5. 1994, Thousand Oaks, CA. USA: Sage Publications.

To address these aspects of the research, different qualitative methods were required. A Yin-based (1994) case study was evaluated and selected as a strategy. This was coupled with a Susman and Evered (1978) action research approach. While direct intervention was not an objective of this investigation, - given the researcher's participant observational role - it was acknowledged the potential was there for it to take place. In these circumstances, action research was viewed as a supplementary strategy which could effectively address such situations.

## 2.4 Case Study Approach

Once the variables and issues impacting on the performance and operation of the virtual software testing teams were identified, the researcher needed to address how and why these had occurred. The case study is defined as particularly suitable for addressing such "how-and-why" type research questions.[19]

The selection of a Yin-based approach was undertaken on the understanding that while Yin's work was a primer, it was also "*an excellent introductory text that developed guidelines for conducting case research. Yin offers much advice to those approaching case study research for experienced as well as novice researchers*".[20] While a Yin-based case study is normally considered a positivist qualitative research approach, its selection for this research was only made once it was clear that it could be legitimately implemented utilising an exploratory strategy (see Section 2.4.3).

All empirical studies have an implicit or an explicit research design. Yin (1994) defines research design as "*an action plan for getting from here to there*". (For the purposes of this volume, the term *here* is defined as the initial research questions and *there* as the conclusions reached.) Central to the design of an efficient research plan was the need to put structures in place that would ensure that the research remained focused on its fundamental goals and objectives. The motivation for this research was that it should be carried out in an ideographic manner, one which embarks on a journey of discovery that remains bounded in its relevant context while not being constrained by it. This approach allowed topics, issues

---

[19] Yin, R.K., Case study research / design and methods Second ed. Applied Social Research Methods Vol. 5. 1994, Thousand Oaks, CA. USA: Sage Publications.
[20] Dutton, W.H., Letters to the Editor. MIS Quarterly, 1988. 12(4): p. 521.

and relevant areas which were grounded in the data to emerge. It also facilitated the researcher in identifying areas worthy of further investigation, areas which are sometimes beyond the scope of this specific research project.

### 2.4.1 The Components of Research Design

When developing a design for undertaking case-study based research five relevant components ought to be addressed:

1. The study's questions.
2. Its propositions, if any.
3. The unit(s) of analysis.
4. The logic linking the data to the postpositions.
5. The criteria for interpreting the findings.

These components were used where applicable as the basis for the research design implemented in the case study presented for this work.

### 2.4.2 The Development of Study Questions

The first step in developing effective research questions is the identification and selection of the research problem.
This has been defined in Chapter one as follows:

> The identification of the key factors, infrastructure, methods, process and procedures, which facilitate and hinder effective globally distributed software virtual team testing.

The next step was the development and phrasing of the original research question, thereby summarizing the problem area selected. The original research question for this volume was formally defined as follows:

> How can software testing in a globally distributed virtual team environment be carried out effectively?

This question was deliberately pitched at a high level of abstraction and is the precursor to the development of more specific questions. An important element in the identification and selection of additional research questions was that they should be broad enough to facilitate discovery, while remaining centred on the research problem. This juxtapositional approach was required so as to provide an effective framework within which the research could be undertaken. The goal here was to determine *how* virtual team members functioned and *how* they performed (collectively) as operational teams. This was coupled with the requirement to identify the variables, factors and relationships which directly or indirectly impacted on operational performance and on the operation of the teams as a whole. Once identified, the research needed to address *how* and *why* these various variables and factors had such an effect. This took place in the context of the initial literature review and the research gap it had identified. Based on these criteria the research questions were defined as follows:

- How is globally distributed virtual team software testing carried out within the division of the organisation researched?
- What areas of virtual team testing have been successfully undertaken and how and why have they been successful?
- What problems (if any) do the virtual teams experience and how are they addressed?
- What problems (if any) have not been addressed and why?
- How and why do problems arise and how do they impact on the operation of the teams?
- What are the key objectives and variables that need to be addressed in order to develop and facilitate GSD virtual team software testing?
- Is software testing a simple activity that can easily be off-shored?
- Is virtual team software testing different to virtual team software development and, if it is, how and why are these differences manifested?
- What can this investigation add to the body of existing knowledge regarding globally distributed virtual team software testing and to GSD in general?

### 2.4.3 Study Propositions

The second component of case-study based research design, as outlined by Yin, (1994) is the development of study propositions. Each proposition is defined as a mechanism for directing the researcher's attention to specific areas, areas which should be focused on within the scope of this study. This approach allows the researcher to develop theories prior to undertaking the research in order to envisage what the possible outcomes of the investigation might be.

Yin goes on to recognise that when undertaking exploratory case-study research there is a legitimate reason for not having pre-developed propositions and states:

> "At the same time some studies may have a legitimate reason for not having any propositions… in which a topic is a subject of 'exploration'".

Due consideration as to what determined the success (or otherwise) of this research investigation was required from the outset, however. The overall objectives of the research needed to be focused from the off and its success determined by the achievement of these same objectives.[21] This approach did not pre-empt any of the findings which the research might generate. This approach was also broad enough to explore what might constitute success, however.

### 2.4.4 Unit Of Analysis

The definition of the term "unit of analysis" refers to the focus of this research and (therefore) what is defined as the case. Creswell (1994) characterises a case study as an entity or phenomenon bounded by time and activity, an entity which can be based on either individual or group approaches. The focus for this research project was identified as the operational and group activities of the staff and management of Computing World (Ireland) Ltd. – as engaged in globally distributed virtual team software testing.

A single case study was the most effective method to employ in this investigation. The rationale for selecting this approach was that it offered the opportunity to study what Yin (1994) terms a revelatory case. This case study also provided the opportunity to research aspects of virtual team software development which had not been investigated before. These included the operations of both management and staff, many of whom had extensive co-site testing experience and had also participated in projects where work was outsourced or off-shored to them. Both groups were now off-shoring their work to remote colleagues in the context of participating in virtual teams. These individuals had extensive experience of dealing with globally-distributed teams and personnel, but not within a virtual team context.

It was of particular interest to identify whether the experience gained while being outsourced or off-shored to - would have any bearing on how these workers operated as virtual team members. This was

---

[21] Yin, R.K., Case study research / design and methods Second ed. Applied Social Research Methods Vol. 5. 1994, Thousand Oaks, CA. USA: Sage Publications.

considered a new and unique opportunity to gain new insights into the complex processes of virtual software team operation. Yin (1994) points out that the "vulnerability" of a single case study must be reflected upon in order to minimise the possibility of misrepresentation. There needs to be ample opportunity to access and collect the necessary case study data. Only when both of these issues have been satisfactorily addressed, can an effective single case study strategy be initiated.

Based on the scope of the research questions outlined here and the review of the operations of the test department of Computing World (Ireland) Ltd., it was determined that two embedded subunits of analysis were required. This equated to the operation of two virtual teams within the testing department. It was decided for anonymity's sake to name these respective teams - the Alpha team and the Beta team. The Alpha team had already been in operation with its virtual team members for over a year-and-a-half, while the Beta team had been operating with virtual team members for a period of six months. These two units of analysis were typical of the testing department as a whole and were the primary – albeit not exclusive - focus for this research project.

At this juncture, it is important to note that the data from the two units of analysis under-research demonstrated very few differences in terms of the results which emerged. This was a completely unexpected outcome given the difference in how long each team had been established. What differences there were will be discussed in further detail - in Chapter nine.

### 2.4.5 The Logic Linking the Data to the Propositions

In a Yin-based case study, the two research design components – i.e. the logic linking the data to the propositions and the criteria for interpreting the findings – are inter-related. Both components are linked to the data analysis stage of the case study. As a result of the exploratory nature of the strategy implemented in this initial investigation, the findings began to emerge from the data. Rather than linking the emergent data to the propositions, there was a requirement to link the data with the overall purpose and objectives of this research (see Section 2.4.3).

### 2.4.6 The Criteria for Interpreting The Findings

Given the exploratory nature of this research, the results needed to be interpreted, verified and placed in-context. To achieve this objective, the results which emerged from the data analysis were triangulated with existing research in the areas of virtual team operation, GSD, Software Process Improvement (SPI) project management practice and, related aspects of organisational theory.

## 2.5 Action Research

Action research was the second and supplementary research methodology selected to deal specifically with the interventionist aspects of undertaking participant observational research. Action research is a variant of quasi-experimental research. It entails analysing the researcher's direct intervention.[22]

The primary difference between action research and other forms of research is the collaborative nature of the relationship between the 'client' and the researcher. Agreement between both is required at each milestone of the project. "*Contracting in action research is generally described as psychological, as motives, goals and the locus of control, as well as business arrangements, are all carefully discussed and agreed*".[23] Such collaboration ensures acceptance of the definition of the problem and the solution which is proposed.

Action research consists of a five-phase cyclical, process-based approach as defined by Susman and Evered (1978). This five-phase cyclical process-based approach is defined as follows:

The client-system infrastructure is established and is then followed by:

- Diagnosis
- Action Planning
- Action Taking
- Evaluation
- Specify Learning

[22] Gill, J. and P. Johnson, Research Methods for Managers, ed. Second. 1997, London UK.

[23] Gill, J. and P. Johnson, Research Methods for Managers, ed. Second. 1997, London UK.

This model defines an iterative cycle approach, see Figure 2.4 for a graphical view of the model.

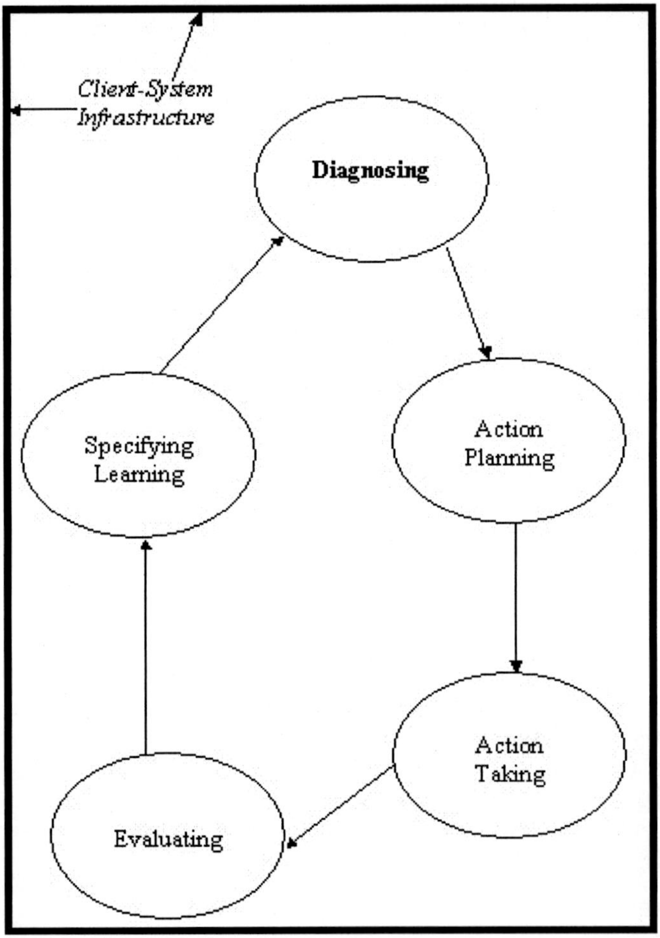


Figure 2.4: The Action Research Cycle (Baskerville, 1999)

The client-system infrastructure is the collaborative agreement reached between the client and the researcher, an agreement which defines the boundaries of the research area. The initial *diagnosis* phase is where the underlying causes and reasons for change are collaboratively defined. In the *action planning* phase the activities required to bring about that change are collaboratively planned. This is followed by the *action taking* phase where the planned actions are carried out.

A collaborative *evaluation* is carried out and the effectiveness of the actions employed are researched. This is followed by the "*specify learning*" phase where the lessons learned from the activities (as a whole) are directed to the client. The client may utilise this information to amend the organisational norms so as to reflect this knowledge or to assist with further process improvements. It is also utilised by the researcher as part of the research programme when it is used to evaluate and validate the research that has already been carried out.

## 2.6 Data Analysis

To cater for the exploratory aspects of this investigation - as incorporated within the case-study based approach that has been selected - there was a need for an inductive strategy. Having researched various alternatives, a grounded theory approach was selected as the most appropriate method for data collection and analysis.

Grounded theory has evolved into two separate approaches to theory building - i.e. what Ezzy (2002) defines as the simplistic inductive model and the sophisticated model. Both of these approaches reflect the divergent views of their originators - Barney Glaser and Anselm Strauss - while both also remain based on their joint work. Strauss's evolved approach to grounded theory initially appeared in Strauss and Corbin (1990) while Glaser's challenge to this work was presented in *The Basics of Grounded Theory Analysis: Emergence vs Forcing* (1992) - where he outlined his own theoretical approach and the differences between the two methods.

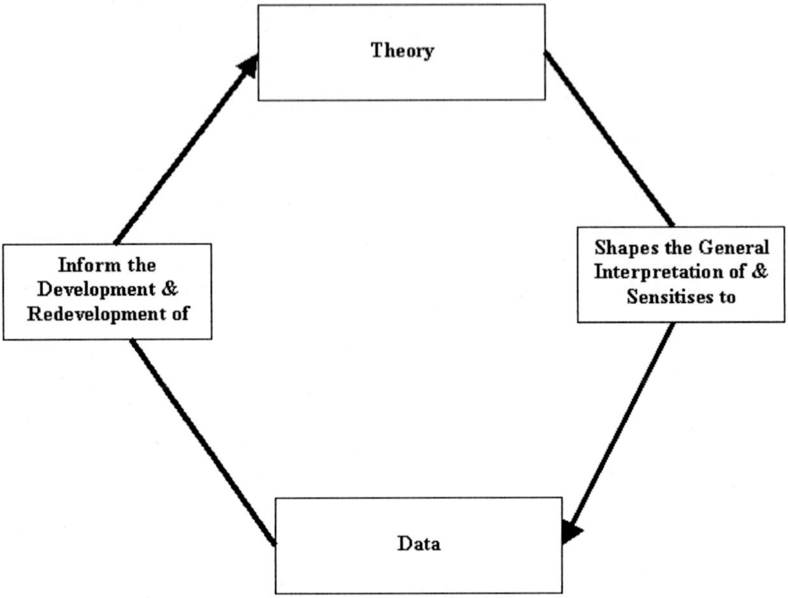


Figure 2.5: Grounded Theory: A Sophisticated Model[24]

Glaser championed what is termed the simplistic grounded theory approach (see Figure 2.2), whereby research is undertaken with as few predetermined ideas as possible. According to Glaser (1992): "*the dictum in grounded theory research is: There is a need not to review any of the literature in the substantive area under study*". Glaser goes on to state: "*Qualitative research cannot produce a grounded theory. It produces a forced, preconceived, full conceptual description*". Glaser's view is that this approach to grounded theory outlined also involves the "*preconceived forcing of data*".[25]

In the sophisticated grounded theory model (see Figure 2.5), it is recognised that the researcher can bring a considerable background in

[24] Ezzy, D., Qualitative Analysis Practice and Innovation. 2002, London UK: Routledge.
[25] Glaser, B.G., The Basics of Grounded Theory Analysis : Emergence vs Forcing. 1992, Mill Valley, CA. USA: Sociology Press.

professional and disciplinary literature to the research project.[26] This acknowledges the role of pre-existing theory (background knowledge and the literature) in '*sensitising*' the researcher towards addressing specific questions and issues. It is very important to stress that this is not hypothesis-formulation or testing. Ezzy (2002) goes on to highlight this point by quoting

> "Consistent with the logic of grounded theory, this study did not begin with any explicit hypothesis testing. Instead we began with broad sensitizing questions..."[27]

There is a distinct difference between sensitising and theorising questions. While previous subject-related experience including the literature review should be used to sensitise the researcher in orienting research questions on specific areas, pre-existing theory should not be allowed to constrain what is discovered. In this context (Strauss and Corbin, 1998) raises relevant questions with reference to the concepts which appear in the data:

> "Are these concepts truly emergent, or am I seeing these concepts in the data because I am so familiar with them? If they are truly emergent and relevant, then how are they the same as/different from those, in the literature?"

The primary goal in implementing a grounded theory based strategy was to approach this investigation with as open a mind as possible. The researcher had prior professional experience in virtual team operation and knowledge of the literature. This research was necessary in order to facilitate the generation of theories grounded in the data produced. It was therefore necessary to develop and implement the key characteristics of a sophisticated grounded theorist as outlined in (Strauss and Corbin, 1998):

- The ability to step back and critically analyse situations.
- The ability to recognize the tendency toward bias.
- The ability to think abstractly.
- The ability to be flexible and open to helpful criticism.
- Sensitivity to the work and the actions of the respondents.
- A sense of absorption in and devotion to the work process.

---

[26] Strauss, A. and J. Corbin, Basics of Qualitative Research : Techniques and Procedures for Developing Grounded Theory. Second ed. 1998, Thousand Oaks, CA, USA: Sage Publications.

[27] Karp, D.A., L.L. Holmstrom, and P.S. Gray, Leaving home for college: Expectations for selective reconstruction of self. Symbolic Interaction, 1998. 21(3): p. 253-276.

These approaches were implemented when and where possible during the course of this research.

### 2.6.1 The Justification for the Selection of Grounded Theory

The primary benefit of selecting grounded theory was that it provided an effective strategy for undertaking explorative research for this project. The following question had to be asked – i.e. whether there was a need for an exploratory approach? After all, there was some literature already published on the operation of virtual teams, project management and GSD when this research was first initiated. The factors which made this investigation different were those which related to the discovery of new aspects and new approaches to this subject area. The research approach outlined here permitted the investigation of management operations and the operations of those staff who had extensive experience of having work off-shored to them. They were now responsible for off-shoring part of what, up to that point, had been their own work - to remote colleagues. They also had to work closely with these colleagues within a virtual team context. In addition to this, software testing in the virtual team and GSD settings was seen as a straightforward task - and it was important to determine whether that was the case. The implementation of a grounded theory approach provided a particularly effective method to investigate these situations.

While action research (as stated in Section 2.5) was used to deal with the interventionist aspects of this investigation, the benefits of utilising a grounded theory approach in conjunction with action research have also been recognised.

## 2.7 Industrial Experience and the Literature Review: Some Issues

The researcher had acted as a professional consultant in the area of software testing during the course of his previous position in industry. He also had four years experience as a Software Quality Manager in an Irish-based company which was partnered with a financial organisation located in the USA. This partnership maintained bespoke financial software, utilising a virtual software team development strategy between both the USA and Ireland. The researcher had also carried out and published research based on the operation of these virtual teams. In implementing a grounded theory based strategy, previous work should not hinder or constrain any current research. The goal rather is to allow the results from this investigation to speak for themselves and - where possible – allow them enhance our existing knowledge of virtual team testing software. When employing a grounded theory approach it is recommended that "*the researcher does not want to be so steeped in the literature that he or she is constrained or stifled by it*".[28] The authors qualify this statement, however, by asserting that a "*state of complete objectivity is impossible*". In this volume the principal researcher utilised his knowledge of GSD, testing and the virtual team literature to identify some initial gaps in the research. The objective then was to utilise this knowledge and experience with sensitivity during the research phase so as not to be constrained or blinded by it.

Initially, the researcher's approach sought to maintain independence from the data and to think comparatively by comparing various aspects of the data. The second research approach was to seek the views of employees at different levels of the organisation and (thirdly) to use multiple sources for data gathering. It was found necessary to "step back" on numerous occasions during the research and say "*What is going on here?*" and "*How do the conclusions reached in this situation fit with the rest of the data as a whole?*" – in order to enhance our overview of the research process as a whole.

## 2.8 The Benefits Of Case Study Research Design

To inaugurate the onsite aspect of this investigation, an initial meeting was held with a senior member of the technical staff in Computing (Ireland) Ltd where the proposed research was outlined. After the submission of a written research proposal a meeting was held with three members of the management of Computing World (Ireland) Ltd., where the proposal was agreed.

The most appropriate method to facilitate effective data collection within this case study was the adoption of a participant observation approach. This was coupled with document review, interviews, questionnaire completion and focus groups. The on-site aspects of the research allowed

[28] Strauss, A. and J. Corbin, Basics of Qualitative Research : Techniques and Procedures for Developing Grounded Theory. Second ed. 1998, Thousand Oaks, CA, USA: Sage Publications.

first-hand participant observation of the teams engaged in their various day-to-day activities – and across a number of telecommunication technologies. It was agreed that the researcher ought to be located on-site in the Computing World (Ireland) Ltd. plant on a full-time basis – for a period of four to five months. The exact duration of time on-site depended on how long it would take before the data saturation point was reached.

## 2.9 The Case Study Research Protocol

Utilising a case study[29], action research[30] approach and grounded theory[31] strategy it was realised each of these approaches has its own strengths and weaknesses. The rationale for implementing a joint strategy was to capitalise on the strengths which they provided.

The research design was utilised as the basis for the development of a simple case study protocol. This protocol provided an overview of the various research objectives. It identified the sources of the data and briefly outlined the procedure for information-information. It detailed the research questions as defined in the research design and also outlined the proposed analysis method which would be employed. Yin (1994) states that a research protocol increases the reliability of case-study based investigation and should be utilised as a guide for undertaking this type of research.

## 2.10 Data Sources

Yin (1994) outlines three principles for data collection in order to achieve the objectives of validity and reliability:

- Use multiple sources of evidence.
- Create a case study database.
- Maintain a chain of evidence.

The selection of documentation review, direct observation, group discussions, interviews and questionnaires all ensured diverse sources for

[29] Yin, R.K., Case study research / design and methods Second ed. Applied Social Research Methods Vol. 5. 1994, Thousand Oaks, CA. USA: Sage Publications.
[30] Susman, G. and R. Evered, An Assessment of the Scientific Merits of Action Research. The Administrative Science Quarterly, 1978. 23(4): p. 582 -603.
[31] Strauss, A. and J. Corbin, Basics of Qualitative Research : Techniques and Procedures for Developing Grounded Theory. Second ed. 1998, Thousand Oaks, CA, USA: Sage Publications.

data collection. These were considered adequate to address the principle of multiple sources of evidence. To create and manage data for the case study, the database "*The Personal Brain*" produced by the Technologies Corporation was selected. This database provided a dynamic front-end environment in which data and analysis could be linked and laid out in a logical manner for prompt retrieval. A reliable chain of evidence was also maintained. Grounded theory "*provides a high degree of rigor and embodies a multi-threaded chain of evidence that is important in achieving reliability in qualitative research*".[32] A detailed analysis of the data – both at the micro and macro levels - was also undertaken. This included concept-level, intermediate-level and high-level category identification.

## 2.11 Participant Observation

The on-site aspect of the investigations commenced on the 3rd of February 2004 - in Computing World (Ireland) Ltd. A participant observation-based approach was adopted to undertake the on-site aspect of this investigation. This was a key element of the research process as it provided the basis for all other aspects of the data gathering and analysis process. The case study, action research and grounded theory approaches lend themselves to a participant or direct research strategy.

> "A case study is an empirical inquiry that investigates a contemporary phenomenon within its real-life context".[33]

> "The ideal domain of action research methods is characterized by… the researcher is actively involved".[34]

> "A good way to begin is to do some initial interviews and observations".[35]

Participant observation is defined as:

---

32 Baskerville, R.L. and J. Pries-Heje, Grounded Action Research: A Method for Understanding IT in Practice. Accounting, Management and Information Technologies, 1999. 9(1): p. 1-23.

33 Yin, R.K., Case study research / design and methods Second ed. Applied Social Research Methods Vol. 5. 1994, Thousand Oaks, CA. USA: Sage Publications.

34 Baskerville, R.L., Investigating Information Systems with Action Research Communications of the Association for Information Systems, 1999(2): p. Article 19.

35 Strauss, A. and J. Corbin, Basics of Qualitative Research : Techniques and Procedures for Developing Grounded Theory. Second ed. 1998, Thousand Oaks, CA, USA: Sage Publications.

> "the sustained immersion of the researcher among those who (sic) he or she seeks to study with a view to generating a rounded in-depth account of the group".[36]

The advantage offered by the direct participant observation approach in this research project was the opportunity it provided to experience first hand the day-to-day activities[37] of the Computing World testing teams. The role of the researcher was to observe these activities as a participant. The objective was to utilise this opportunity to systematically collect relevant data for analysis. To achieve this goal, initial activities which were undertaken included a document and infrastructural review - as combined with direct observation. This was followed by the preparation of interview questions and the selection of interview participants. Agreement was reached with the relevant Project Managers and two focus groups were organised. To supplement and expand on the data, questionnaires were also prepared. Interviews were carried out, focus groups were held, and the questionnaires were completed and returned. At all stages of this process, a direct observational approach was implemented. This under-pinned all of the on-site aspects of the investigation.

Yin (1994) states potential bias as a major danger to the participant observational strategy – a danger that can manifest itself in three specific ways:

- The researcher has less opportunity to operate as an external observer.
- The researcher may become a supporter of the group or the organisation.
- The researcher takes up too much time participating and does not have enough time to research.

During his period in Computing World (Ireland) Ltd. the principal researcher was cognisant of the relevance of each of these factors and endeavoured to avoid the dangers as highlighted.

---

[36] Bryman, A., Quantity and Quality in Social Research Contemporary Social Research, ed. M. Blumer. Vol. 18. 1988, London: Routledge.

[37] Gerson, K. and R. Horowitz, Observation and Interviewing, in Qualitative Research in Action, T. May, Editor. 2002, Sage: London.

## 2.12 Documentation And Infrastructure Review

As a precursor to undertaking the documentation and infrastructural review, time was spent with the Test Process subject-matter expert (SME) who provided a high-level overview of the test operation and its processes. Information regarding the existence and location of relevant documentation was also supplied.

### 2.12.1 Document Review

The objectives of undertaking the documentation review were:

- To gain an understanding of the structure and activities of the test operations in the organisation .
- To obtain a knowledge of the testing process as documented.
- To determine roles and responsibilities.
- To determine the completeness, clarity and availability of relevant documentation.
- To use the documented process as a basis to evaluate practice.
- To determine if documentation was used by the testers or if it was shelf-ware.
- To use the documentation to augment other sources of evidence.

An extensive review of the process documentation was carried out. This incorporated the artefacts created to coordinate various projects and those generated as part of the testing process. The documents reviewed included:

- Formal Process Procedures.
- Organisational And Divisional Intranet Web Sites.
- Project Plans.
- Test Management Plans.
- Feature Test Plans.
- Feature Test Strategy Documents.
- Test Cases.

The review of the process documentation provided a comprehensive overview of the test activities and the structure of the department, thereby enabling the researcher to gain a theoretical, low-level knowledge of the testing process. This knowledge was essential when determining actual practice and when compared with the documented methodology. It also allowed the content and clarity of the process documentation to be evaluated.

### 2.12.2 Infrastructure Review

The infrastructure provided to support the operation of the virtual testing teams was reviewed. The objective of this review was to determine:

- What infrastructure was in place?
- How that infrastructure was utilized?
- Was this infrastructure adequate to meet the needs of virtual teams?

This review was carried out through both direct observation and informal interviews with the Test Process SME, the Team Members and the Management. This subject was also explored in the focus groups and in the in-depth interviews.

## 2.13 The Interview Process

This research project centred on the Irish-based virtual team members of the test operation, focusing on the specific day-to-day activities of two of these teams. The opportunity to undertake research directly with the Far Eastern virtual team members would have been useful at this point but access was not made available and it was therefore beyond the scope of this research project.

### 2.13.1 Preparations for the Interview Phase

The interview is one of the most important sources of information in case study based research.[38] Preparations for the interview phase therefore warranted considerable time and effort.[39] An equal number of participants were interviewed in the two teams studied. All interviews had to be fully leveraged to ensure that the best use was made of the time and the resources provided by the interviewee and the company. Interviews were of one-hour duration with provision for an extra thirty minutes, if required. The interview phase of this investigation could only be completed when the data saturation point had been achieved.

---

[38] Yin, R.K., Case study research / design and methods Second ed. Applied Social Research Methods Vol. 5. 1994, Thousand Oaks, CA. USA: Sage Publications.

[39] Gerson, K. and R. Horowitz, Observation and Interviewing, in Qualitative Research in Action, T. May, Editor. 2002, Sage: London.

The document review and the participant observation research already undertaken had highlighted a number of areas which required further investigation. Semi-structured interviews were now employed, through the use of open-ended questions which focused discussion in the relevant areas while not constraining the research investigation. This allowed for the clarification and development of a deeper knowledge and understanding of various subject areas while also providing the opportunity for new and relevant data/issues to emerge.

The development of the GSD questionnaire also helped address this phase of the research process. Where pre-identified salient topics could not be discussed during the interview, they could be adequately addressed by completion of the questionnaire. The overall objective here was not to lead the interviewees – but rather to facilitate them in expressing their own insights, views and experiences of the operations and activities of the virtual team to which they belonged.

### 2.13.2 Development of The Semi-Structured Interview

A generic outline was prepared for the semi-structured interviews. Extensive use was made of the mind-mapping technique[40] during this exercise. The generic nature of this approach meant that it was broad enough to cover all of the interviewee roles and experiences. Flexibility required that room be left where additional areas could be added and others removed when circumstances dictated. This had to take place in a structured but flexible environment, in a sensitive manner which facilitated and fostered effective communication. The areas identified for further investigation provided the structure for this process. This structure was then incorporated into the interview format so as to use these various issues and questions as a catalyst for discussion.

## 2.14 The Questionnaire

The interview process was supplemented by the completion of a questionnaire so as to provide an additional data source. After each interview, the respondent was requested to complete the questionnaire and return it within a two-week period. The objective in utilising the questionnaire was to provide a mechanism which allowed the interviewees

[40] Gerson, K. and R. Horowitz, Observation and Interviewing, in Qualitative Research in Action, T. May, Editor. 2002, Sage: London.

the opportunity - after a period of reflection - to expand on and/or clarify issues which were raised during their interview.

It also provided the researcher with flexibility when a respondent raised additional relevant areas of interest. In these circumstances, there was no need to constrain the discussion as the researcher was aware that the respondent would also complete the questionnaire.

### 2.14.1 The Preparation of the GSD Questionnaire

Considerable reflection and effort went into the design and content of the questionnaire. Gill and Johnson (1997) outline the following steps for developing a questionnaire format:

- Focus.
- Phraseology.
- Necessary form of response.
- Sequencing and general presentation.

These steps were all incorporated into the questionnaire design.

The focus of a questionnaire is defined as "*the extent to which the questions ... cover the various aspects of the research problem*".[41] Key issues highlighted in the research which had been undertaken up to that point were incorporated into the questionnaire. The term "phraseology" refers to the way in which the questions are asked. The approach employed here was to ask open-ended questions which could be used as a mechanism for the respondent to provide as much relevant information as possible.

The form of each response to the questionnaire was determined by the five different types of questions employed:

- Direct questions which required a one-line answer.
- Questions which required the selection of a "yes" or "no" answer.
- Selection from a list that best described the respondent's experience.
- Open-ended questions that focused on eliciting a detailed response.
- Questions that required an ordinal response regarding personal preference.

---

[41] Gill, J. and P. Johnson, Research Methods for Managers, ed. Second. 1997, London UK.

The problems associated with having respondents complete large questionnaires were considered from the very beginning.[42] The size of the questionnaire was restricted to three pages of questions with a blank page for additional comments. The objective here was to necessitate a maximum completion time of forty-five minutes. This proved a very successful approach and a one hundred percent response rate for questionnaire completion was achieved.

A generic questionnaire was initially prepared and then tailored to the specific roles of the respondents - so that only questions that were deemed relevant were asked. Due to staff time and work constraints, the questionnaire respondents were restricted to the interviewees and the questionnaire was developed accordingly.

## 2.15 Focus Groups

The two Project Managers approached the researcher separately to request that he facilitate group meetings with their Irish-based team members. The objective of these meetings was to discuss virtual team operation and how it could be improved. These requests linked in directly with the researcher's desire to hold focus group discussions. A date and a duration time of one-and-a-half hours for each focus group was agreed with each of the respective Project Managers.

### 2.15.1 Preparation for the Focus Groups

For the focus groups a presentation was prepared based on the results derived from direct observation, the documentation, the infrastructural review and the analysis of the interviews that had been undertaken. The topics covered by the presentation were:

- Communication.
- Culture.
- Trust.
- Coordination.

The objective of the presentation was to raise relevant topics for consideration and to stimulate further discussion. Whilst these topics were a catalyst, it was important to ensure that there was room for additional or

---

[42] Burchell, B. and C. Marsh, The Effect of Questionnaire Length on Survey Response. Quality and Quantity 1992 26 (3): p. 233 - 244.

relevant subject areas to be explored. The researcher chaired the discussion and noted salient points as and when they arose.

The schedule for both focus groups was as follows:

- Presentation - 15 minutes.
- Discussion - 65 minutes.
- Summary and Conclusion - 10 minutes.

## 2.16 Recording Interviews

Two methods of recording the interviews were selected. The primary method was electronic audio recording. The secondary method involved handwritten notes. Inevitably, there were limitations to both approaches. Respondents had to agree to have their interview electronically recorded. There was also the possibility that the participants would agree to this and yet find themselves constrained in their discussion as a result of the operation of the recording devices. On the other hand, the handwritten option was very slow and could not be utilised to record all of the ongoing discourse. When it came to the interviews all of the respondents agreed to have them recorded.

It was difficult to determine exactly to what extent the electronic recording of the interviews constrained the interviewees in their responses. What emerged from the analysis of the data, however, was the level of candour demonstrated in their interviews. This point was illustrated by a respondent who stated they would not share their knowledge with their remote colleagues. The seriousness of such a statement was understood and followed by the words: "*testing one, two, three, testing*". The implication was clear – i.e. the respondent was saying - I know you are taping this interview, but here is what I think anyway. The handwritten notes were utilised to clarify the audio recording when required.

## 2.17 Selection of the Interview Participants

During the on-site aspect of this investigation it was decided that four people would be interviewed from each of the teams which constituted the units of analysis for this case study. The roles of the interviewees were determined by the researcher but the individuals were selected by Management. It was also agreed that the Test Manager, Trainer and the Process SME/Trainer would be interviewed.

Each individual agreed to take part in an in-depth interview lasting a minimum of one hour. The Test Manager also agreed to be interviewed and four interviews where held with him during the on-site aspect of this research.

Prior to the closure of the Computing World (Ireland) Ltd. plant in Ireland, the same Project Managers agreed to be interviewed again. The objective here was to review the various research findings and receive an update on the status of their respective projects. The opportunity also arose to interview a Senior Engineer who was an expert in the testing process and discuss the findings of the investigation with him. These interviews were of particular relevance given that the test operation was being totally transferred to Asia and the Irish-based plant was being closed.

## 2.18 Conducting the Interviews

The generic structure developed for the interviews was reviewed in detail and amended to meet the specific roles of each interviewee. Particular sections were added, deleted or amended as a result of findings from previous interviews.

To address the specific needs of the two units of the case study analysis, a different focus was placed on the questions as addressed to both teams. The focus of the questions for the Alpha team, a team which had over eighteen month's experience of virtual team operation, was: "*what have you learned?*" This was refined into questions like: "*What do you know now about establishing, operating and participating in a virtual team that you would have liked to have known a year and a half ago?*"

The focus of the questions for the Beta team, a team with six months experience of virtual team operation, were of a more general nature. *"What was you experience so far? What are you areas of concern? What was going well and where had problems been experienced?"*

During the interviews an ethical approach and the need for informed consent was of paramount consideration.[43] On commencing each interview, the overall objectives of the research were outlined and the confidential nature of the interview was also reiterated. When relevant

---

[43] Gomm, R., Social Research Methodology: A Critical Introduction. 2004, Basingstoke Palgrave Macmillan.

issues were identified they were incorporated into subsequent interviews for further investigation, when the time constraints allowed.

Similar preparations for the three additional interviews which took place in March of that year were undertaken. The objective here was to determine the overall successes and failures of each project. At that stage both projects had delivered their respective products. In addition, it was considered important to discuss the findings from this research with the Project Managers and the Senior Engineer and to discuss their experiences of implementing the virtual team software testing strategy.

## 2.19 Grounded Theory Based Analysis

The objective of undertaking grounded theory based analysis was to derive concepts and categories which provided a theoretical explanation for the studied phenomena. A creative and scientific approach is an essential element in implementing a grounded theory-based strategy. To develop and promote creativity, Strauss and Corbin (1998) quote and abridge nine out of the ten common themes that provide guidance for creative thinking as outlined in (Patton Quinn, 1990):

1. Being open to multiple possibilities.
2. Generating a list of options.
3. Exploring various possibilities before choosing any one.
4. Making use of multiple avenues of expression.
5. The use of nonlinear forms of thinking.
6. Diverging from the usual way of thinking and working.
7. Trusting the process and not holding back.
8. Putting effort into the work and not taking shortcuts.
9. Having fun while doing it.

One common creative theme which Strauss and Corbin did not include in their list was "making linkages". The objective of this theme is to connect the seemingly unconnected through the use of matrices.[44] The scientific aspect of this data analysis process was addressed by maintaining rigour and grounding the analysis in the data. Strauss and Corbin (1998) go on to outline how creativity is expressed by making sense of the data in the following manner.

---

[44] Patton Quinn, M., Qualitative Evaluation and Research Methods Second ed. 1990, London: Sage.

- The naming of categories.
- Asking stimulating questions.
- Making comparisons.

Bearing all of these factors in mind, the data analysis was initiated. After the transcription of each of the interviews, microanalysis commenced. This included open coding, axial coding, memo writing, process analysis and selective coding. The analysis of the data is outlined in more detail in chapter four.

## 2.20 The Importance of an Effective Research Strategy

Methodology plays an important role in underpinning and supporting the research process. This investigation had to be carried out within specific constraints. Given the nature and impact of these constraints, the objective was to ensure that the most effective use was made of the opportunities and the resources which were available.

To implement the chosen research strategy effectively, the experience, knowledge and personal bias of the researcher were all considered. The practicality of executing the case study, the action research and the grounded theory based approach has been presented here, and the development of the case study protocol outlined. The interview process and the development of the instruments to support it have also been articulated. The latter included the production of both the semi-structured interview questions and the GSD questionnaire.

The objective of the interview process was to facilitate the expansion and development of the investigation by identifying and clarifying relevant topics as and when they emerged. The need for implementing a flexible approach has already been highlighted. The effort expended in preparing for the interview phase was rewarded by the quality of the results received. Where respondents raised issues that were not directly relevant to the research topic they were politely steered back to the matter in hand. When they provided new and additional experiences and insights into the area under investigation the flexibility to focus on those relevant issues was already in place. An effective strategy for the inductive analysis of the data generated during the course of this investigation - has been outlined.

# CHAPTER THREE

# THE ORGANISATION AND TEAMS

## 3.1 The Organisation

### 3.1.1 The Alpha Team

The Irish-based Alpha team members had an average of five years experience working in the testing department. They were highly-skilled workers with a proven track record of delivering on-time, within budget and to the required performance standards. Their Asian colleagues had limited technical experience for the most part and were mainly graduates or new starts hired from other industries. The addition of new Asian-based team members was taking place on an ongoing basis while the on-site research was taking place. The Alpha team had responsibility for testing the release of a Computing World product for a specific technology. This virtual team had been operating with Irish and Asian-based members for a year-and-a-half when the on-site aspect of this investigation was undertaken.

### 3.1.2 The Beta Team

The Beta virtual team had been established for six months when the on-site research was undertaken. This team was responsible for testing the release of a Computing World product for a specific technology. The Irish-based members of the Beta team had an average of four years experience working as testers in the department. They also had a proven track record of delivering tested products on time, within budget, and up to the requisite performance standards. In contrast to this, their Asian colleagues had limited technical experience and were predominantly new employees hired from other industries or graduates hired directly from college.

## 3.2 Implementation of the Virtual Team Strategy

The testing teams carried out the majority of their testing in Ireland until a year-and-a-half before this study was undertaken. A large percentage of this work had been off-shored to Ireland from North America. There had already been some off-shoring of basic testing from Ireland to a number of Asian countries and the Middle East, but the more technical aspects of the testing process were carried out exclusively in Ireland. The off-shored testing from Ireland was primarily non-technical and repetitive in nature. This minimised the need for communication and cooperation between the Irish-based teams and the teams carrying out this work in other geographical locations.

At that time Computing World (Ireland) Ltd. developed a new strategy for their test operation. Virtual teams were established to undertake future testing. These teams consisted primarily of members located in Ireland and an Asian country. To facilitate this strategy the Asian operation was expanded from sixteen to forty-five testing staff. This figure was projected to increase to ninety before the end of the second year. In Ireland, an embargo was placed on recruiting testing staff and all expansion in personnel in the test teams was limited to the Asian country from then on.

The impetus for the implementation of this strategy was cost-driven. Organisations gain competitive advantage from globalization due to labour arbitrage, which allows reduced costs. Computing World, like its competitors, continued to develop and expand a corporate strategy of leveraging global resources for software development.

The key advantage of implementing a virtual team strategy was that experienced and technically-competent test engineers located in Ireland could be partnered with less expensive test engineers in a specific Asian country. This would reduce costs while maintaining testing rigour and continuing to ensure product quality. Such a strategy also facilitated the opportunity to implement a "follow the sun" approach to product testing, one which could leverage temporal difference to reduce the test cycle time and maximise the efficient use of tools and hardware. The overall objective of this approach – as articulated to the staff - was to allow both locations to be leveraged to their best advantage.

## 3.4 Communication Infrastructure

Every member of the testing staff was provided with a networked PC, an e-mail account and a telephone. All telephones had a voicemail facility, but there were two types of handset in use. One provided a flashing light when a voicemail message had been received and not accessed; the other model of telephone had no external indication that a new voicemail message had been received. The notification mechanism employed by this model was a different dial tone which indicated the presence of a new message.

### 3.4.1 Conference Calls and Telephone Usage

The organisation provided conference call facilities and had the infrastructure in place to support this activity. Conference rooms could be booked on-line and were equipped with audiovisual equipment to facilitate group conference calls and NetMeeting presentations. There was also the facility to take part in conference calls directly from an individual's desk and all staff were supplied with a combined earphone and microphone headset. There were no facilities in place for group or individual video conferencing, however.

The Irish-based team members were not restricted from making business-related international telephone calls. Internal, external and international calls could be directly dialled from staff members' desks. Telephone usage was monitored, but it only became an issue if it was abused.

### 3.4.2 Instant Messenger

An organisational version of Instant Messenger (IM) was provided to all virtual team members. Utilising the IM tool can support question and answer sessions, joint problem solving, improved coordination and social interaction.[1] A key objective of using the IM tool is to address, to some degree, the lack of opportunity for informal communication between globally distributed virtual team members.[2] The problems associated with

---

[1] Herbsleb, J.D., et al. Introducing Instant Messaging and Chat in the Workplace. in In the proceedings of ACM Conference on Human Factors in Computing Systems. 2002. Minneapolis, MN, USA: ACM Press.
Handel, M. and J.D. Herbsleb. What is chat doing in the workplace? in Proceedings of the 2002 ACM conference on Computer supported cooperative work 2002. New Orleans, Louisiana, USA.

the loss of informal communication are understood in the GSD environment (see Grinter and Herbsleb, 1999) The advantages offered by IM lie is its informality which has been defined as "*generally impromptu, brief, context rich and dyadic*".[3]

The overall goal of the use of the IM tool is to provide a mechanism to replicate the type of face-to-face informal communication that takes place in the corridor, the canteen or when calling over to a colleague's desk with a question. The effectiveness of IM also depends on time-zone overlap between sites.[4] Team members both need to be in their respective locations at the same time to communicate using the tool.

### 3.4.3 Process Documentation

The process documentation was held on the organisation's intranet where a documented configuration management system was in place.

### 3.4.4 The Intranet, Wide Area Network and the Internet

The organisational intranet provided access to the process documentation, additional resources and links to testing tools and other repositories. These additional resources also included links to specific groups and technology (intranet) web pages. The majority of these links could be accessed through the main intranet page.

The Asian virtual team members had access to the intranet and were networked with Ireland over a Wide Area Network (WAN). The WAN connection was adequate for the day-to-day activities of the virtual teams – (as outlined earlier, the large test equipment was located in Ireland) – but the bandwidth was not available to allow the Asian virtual team members utilise this equipment to carry out real-time system tests remotely. As a result, the Asian virtual team members carried out subsystem testing using

---

[3] Nardi, B.A., S. Whittaker, and E. Bradner. Interaction and outeraction: instant messaging in action in Proceedings of the 2000 ACM conference on Computer supported cooperative work 2000. Philadelphia, Pennsylvania, United States ACM Press.

[4] Yan, Z. Efficient Maintenance Support in Offshore Software Development: a Case Study on a Global E-Commerce Project. in Proc. of the International Workshop on GSD , International Conference on Software Engineering (ICSE 2004),. 2004. Edinburgh, Scotland.

simulators while the Irish-based staff could carry out full system tests due to their physical proximity to the test equipment.

The onsite aspect of this research commenced on the 2nd of February. Between that date and the of 16th March the initial data gathering and document review took place. This included the preparations for ten in-depth interviews which took place between the 16th of March and the 20th . During this process the generated data was analysed and relevant issues were incorporated into the subsequent interviews. In addition to this, four interviews were held with the Test Manager during this period.

Additional interviews were carried out two years after the completion of the onsite aspect of this investigation.

- Alpha team Project Manager.
- Beta team Project Manager.
- Senior Technical Engineer.

During the on-site investigation two focus groups were held, each focus group lasting for one-and-a-half hours. By the end of May of that year the data saturation point had been reached for the on-site aspect of this research. This equated to the researcher spending eighty-six working days (excluding public holidays) on-site in Computing World (Ireland) Ltd - equalling a total of seven hundred and twenty hours on site.

When the researcher returned to the University of Limerick at the end of the on-site period, the ongoing literature review continued. A more detailed analysis of the data generated from the on-site aspect of this investigation was then undertaken. As a result of this, the findings from this research were further analysed and defined. In June of the following year, the findings were presented to the management of Computing World (Ireland) Ltd. At that meeting, each of the findings was considered and the impact which the "fear factor" was having on the operation of the teams was discussed at length. It was clear the Irish-based management felt they could do very little to address this particular issue at that stage. As a result of this meeting, it was decided that communication was the area that Computing World wished to focus on the most. It was agreed that further research would be carried out on this subject area by another researcher, based on the issues highlighted in this investigation.

The opportunity arose for additional interviews to take place prior to the closure of the Computing World operation in Ireland and three further interviews were held at this point. These provided the opportunity to discuss the findings from the investigation with the Project Managers of the Alpha and Beta teams and review the performance of their respective teams and projects. The opportunity also arose to discuss these issues with a Senior Engineer who was an SPI expert and who had considerable knowledge of the test operation.

## 3.7 Conclusion

In this chapter, the structure of the organisation has been presented. The implementation of the virtual team strategy has been outlined and the infrastructure of the test department as incorporated into the communications infrastructure has also been explored and analysed.

# CHAPTER FOUR

# CONCEPTS AND CATEGORIES

## 4. Deriving Concepts and Categories

Strauss and Corbin (1998) have defined grounded theory based data analysis as comprising description, conceptual ordering and theorising. Description is characterised as telling the story from the respondent's perspective. This is followed by conceptual ordering which is the categorisation of data in accordance with its properties and dimensions. Theorising is the construction of an explanation from the various concepts and categories identified during the conceptual ordering process, a process which is carried out in a systematic manner. This characterised the basis on which the data derived from this investigation was analysed. The interviews and focus groups provided a central focus for this study. The documentation and infrastructural review, direct observation, questionnaire and participant observation all contributed additional data, insights, perspectives and contexts to the areas researched and the concepts and categories derived. An overview of the data-gathering and analysis employed in this study is presented in Figure 4.1.

As a precursor to undertaking the analytical process, the initial activity - on completion of each interview - was to prepare an interview transcript swiftly and accurately. At the earliest opportunity, these interviews were analysed and the salient points identified. Where possible, the issues and topics which emerged were incorporated into the direction and content of the next interview and any subsequent interviews. In this way the data generated by the respondents provided the focus and direction for this investigation.

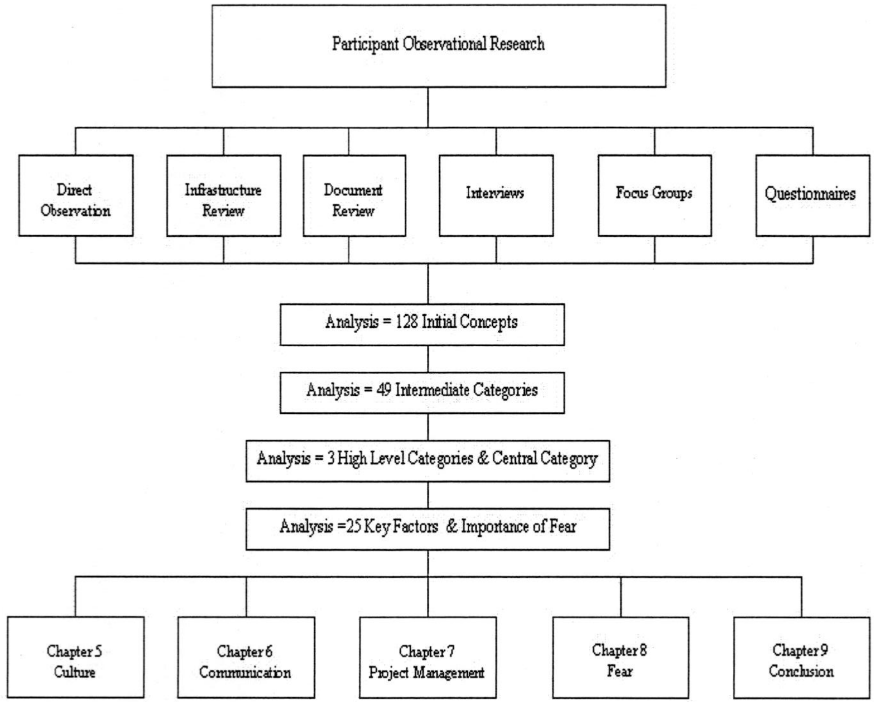


Figure 4.1: Overview of the Collection and Analysis of Data

While grounded theory based analysis is designed to be systematic, it also needs to be implemented "*creatively and flexibly...as considered appropriate*".[1] It is understood that "*it is not a recipe to be applied to research*, but that it offers "*a set of useful tools for analyzing qualitative data"*. It also offers *"a way of thinking about and of viewing the world that can enrich the research of those who chose to use this methodology"*.[2] It was in this context that the analysis of the data was undertaken. While effective, the transcription and analysis of the written word nevertheless has its limitations. Having access to an electronic recording of the interviews allowed the investigator to listen to each interview numerous times during the analysis process. This helped to provide further context and also allowed identification of the use of inflection on certain words and comments.

## 4.1 Microanalysis

The initial task undertaken after transcription was the microanalysis of each interview. Microanalysis is characterised by Strauss and Corbin (1998) as a line-by-line review of the data. The objective here was to identify initial concepts and define their properties and dimensions. It was also to identify relationships between these concepts wherever possible. The data from both focus groups was analysed in a similar manner.

The major aspects of microanalysis are defined as follows:

1. The diverse data gathered and the media utilised to record it.
2. The interpretation of this data by the respondents and the researcher.
3. The recognition by the researcher that it is impossible to be completely objective at all times.

The need to look for and examine alternative explanations and insights was a very important aspect of the analysis process. It was also necessary to view data in the context of the information generated by the research (as a whole) rather than to compartmentalise it in accordance with any preconceived concepts.

---

[1] Strauss, A. and J. Corbin, Basics of Qualitative Research : Techniques and Procedures for Developing Grounded Theory. Second ed. 1998, Thousand Oaks, CA, USA: Sage Publications.

[2] Strauss, A. and J. Corbin, Basics of Qualitative Research : Techniques and Procedures for Developing Grounded Theory. Second ed. 1998, Thousand Oaks, CA, USA: Sage Publications.

A key element of microanalysis is coding. Coding is defined as the process by which data is fractured, conceptualised and integrated to form theory.[3] To this end, an open approach was undertaken to ensure that the research was flexible, creative and systematic. As each line was reviewed the questions asked were:

- What is being expressed here?
- Why is this being articulated in this manner?
- What does this tell me about the individual's perspective, situation, experience and motivation?
- What does it tell me about this person's experience and view of their position, their collocated team members, their remote team members and managers?
- What does being a member of a virtual team mean?
- What hinders or facilitates the operation of the virtual team from this individual's perspective?
- How does this relate to what I know so far?
- What does this confirm or cast doubt on?
- Are there alternative explanations for what is being expressed other than the one that first comes to mind?
- Are the concepts and categories I am identifying actually in the data or am I allowing my past experience and knowledge to misinterpret or distort what is actually there?

The objective here was to define - through questioning and theoretical comparison - the concepts and categories occurring within the data and to determine their properties and dimensions. The overall goal was to gain a better understanding of the data through a combination of both open and axial coding.

### 4.1.1 Open Coding

Open coding was used to uncover, name, and develop those concepts and categories which were evident within the data. This process is termed conceptualising. A concept is defined as a significant phenomenon in the data, one which has been identified and labelled as such. It could be an activity, event, happening, experience, attitude, reaction and/or outlook. Each has recognisable characteristics and dimensions which allow it to be

---

[3] Strauss, A. and J. Corbin, Basics of Qualitative Research: Techniques and Procedures for Developing Grounded Theory. Second ed. 1998, Thousand Oaks, CA, USA: Sage Publications.

abstractly defined and coded. In this way the data is broken down into discrete elements based on similarities and differences.

Similar concepts were identified in the data as based on the sharing of common characteristics and dimensions and as grouped into specific categories. Each category was further defined in terms of common properties and dimensions. What were termed sub-categories were also identified with the objective of determining - how, why and where - certain phenomena was likely to occur. The objective here was to add further clarity and to reduce the data to a more manageable size so that it could be broken down into discernable patterns and variables.

### 4.1.2 Axial Coding

Axial coding is a method to add depth and structure to categories that have been identified in the data. The process is termed "axial" as the coding occurs around the axis of the main categories identified. The definition of axial coding is the process of relating categories to their subcategories. Subcategories, as outlined in section 4.1.1, provide an insight into questions about the categories and the concepts identified. These questions include:

- When, where and why does this phenomenon occur?
- What are the consequences?

The axial coding process as outlined by Strauss and Corbin (1998) is as follows:

1. Laying out the properties and dimensions of a category which takes place during open coding.
2. Identifying the variety of conditions actions/interactions and consequences associated with a phenomenon.
3. Through various statements - relating how categories are related to their subcategories.
4. Looking at the data to determine how major categories are related to each other.

This approach helped provide an insight into the structures and circumstances which facilitated the existence of such categories. It also allowed the identification of activities and interactions that were related to and/or as a result of the phenomena identified. The goal here was to re-assemble the data in a meaningful way so as to gain a better understanding of the phenomena and their internal and external relationships. It also provided an effective basis for building theory. Once initial categories were identified, the process of axial coding could begin. Open coding and axial coding were not necessarily sequential events. They were iterative activities instead, activities which required numerous re-evaluations of the data as the analysis continued.

### 4.1.3 Memos

The practice of writing memos was a key element in the open and axial iterative coding process. In the Grounded Theory context a memo is defined as: "*The researcher's record of analysis, thoughts, interpretations and directions for further data collection*".[4] The role and purpose of the memo was to ensure that it kept the researcher grounded in the data and maintain that awareness throughout the analytical process. Strauss and Corbin (1998) state that one of the major benefits of writing memos is that it forces the researcher to conceptualise. Over 210 pages of memos were prepared during the analysis process.

The practicality of implementing a creative and scientific approach required a line-by-line review of each interview. Each sentence and paragraph was analysed in the light of the questions presented in section 4.1.2. Based on this analysis, memos were written focusing on the most salient points. Diagrams were also prepared and were found to be very useful. The process of identifying concepts and categories and their properties and dimensions was undertaken and refined during additional reviews.

The researcher had made the decision to carry out the analysis of the data in the "*old fashioned way*".[5] This involved the manual identification of concepts and categories which were defined from interview transcripts and focus group notes.

---

[4] Strauss, A. and J. Corbin, Basics of Qualitative Research : Techniques and Procedures for Developing Grounded Theory. Second ed. 1998, Thousand Oaks, CA, USA: Sage Publications.

[5] Strauss, A. and J. Corbin, Basics of Qualitative Research : Techniques and Procedures for Developing Grounded Theory. Second ed. 1998, Thousand Oaks, CA, USA: Sage Publications.

### 4.1.4 The Initial Coding Process

There were two phases to the initial coding process: The first took place when each interview had been transcribed. A basic analysis of each interview, one which included open and axial coding, was undertaken. The objective of this approach was to define the major concepts, categories, properties and dimensions which emerged from the data. Where and when relevant, these issues and topics were incorporated into subsequent interviews and subjected to further analysis. This took the form of identifying and refining relevant questions, making comparisons, and defining and redefining concepts and categories where necessary. Each interview and focus group contained a component of "sensitising" questions. During the interviews and focus groups, the answers to these and subsequent questions played an important role in the identification of the emerging concepts and categories, while the diversity of the respondents' answers also raised further questions for the investigation to focus on and address.

A second stage of the initial coding process was required - given the haste with which the initial transcripts were prepared. The transcripts were rechecked for accuracy. Subsequent corrections were of a minor nature and did not impact on any of the salient points which had emerged from the data. The intention here was effective data capture and analysis. Another key activity was to ensure that it was recognised when the data saturation point was achieved for both units of analysis.

As the interviews and analysis continued, the focus expanded to include the development and refinement of theoretical questions and centred on those of a more practical and structural nature. As a result, there was a requirement for the guiding questions to be developed and amended - from being open-ended to being more specific - as concepts and categories became clearer and their interrelationships became more defined. The type of comparison between emerging concepts and categories which took place as part of the analysis process can be illustrated by the example outlined below:

During the fourth interview, a Team Leader highlighted the difficulties they experienced with the use of "XXXXX", a problem-reporting tool. Because the tool was not being operated correctly and a security feature was being over-ridden it was causing serious problems. When the respondent was asked whether the problem was with the way the tool was operated or the tool itself? - the answer given was: "*It is the tool and the way the tool is used*".

Having outlined the problems the respondent was asked if a process problem report (PR) had been raised on this issue, given the difficulties it had caused. The reply was as follows: *"I have raised this and there are process PRs opened and people are talking about it and that is about it and it's a nightmare"*. Additional details on this specific problem were gained from subsequent questions during the interview, i.e. its cause and its full implications.

When this interview was analysed it was clear that there was a specific problem with the use of the "XXXXX" tool, a problem which warranted further investigation. A direct comparison was made with the data which had been previously collated. It was noted that the difficulties associated with the use of the tool had not been identified during the participant observation. Similarly, problems had not been raised with regard to its use in any of the preceding interviews. As a result, the concept of using an effective problem-reporting tool was extended to consider what difficulties, if any, were associated with the use of the "XXXXX" tool? It was also important to determine how widespread and severe these problems were and what additional areas they might have impacted upon. This question was raised in subsequent interviews with staff on both teams.

In all cases, the respondents did not articulate any particular problems with the tool or its use. It was clear from the analysis that the problems experienced with "XXXXX" were specific to the Team Leader who raised the issue. However, this issue still warranted investigating since it had the potential to be a serious problem for the operation of the teams as a whole. An additional issue was that despite the fact that "XXXXX" and its operation had been identified as a problem, and a process problem report was opened, nothing had been done about it. This also required further investigation. This example highlights how, through analysis, the data was both broken down and expanded upon.

## 4.2 The Development of Categories from Concepts

The saturation point was reached when new concepts were no longer identified from the analysis of the data and those which did emerge only replicated the properties and dimensions of the concepts which had already been acknowledged. Having carried out a transcription review and a coding analysis, an additional review was required to develop the concepts and categories further. Each interview was again reviewed and analysed by reading the transcripts and listening to the recordings. The purpose here was to get a clear understanding of what was being said and how it was expressed in the context of the interviews and the data generated for direct observation. Additional, open and axial coding took place. This allowed the initial concepts to be further developed and laid the framework for the creation of the contact summary sheets.

### 4.2.1 The Preparation of the Contact Summary Sheets

As part of the axial coding process, the preparation of contact summary sheets was of particular value in the development of the intermediate categories. The task of creating a contact summary sheet for each interview had two advantages: Firstly, it allowed the researcher to consider what were the main concepts, questions and issues that arose during each interview. This prevented them getting lost in the detail of the data. The preparation of contact summary sheets allowed relevant concepts to be combined, named, and categorised effectively for each specific interview.

A second goal was to summarise the intermediate categories for each interview. The contact summary sheet provided a comprehensive medium in which to present a concise synopsis of this information. This was then sorted into relevant groups. The process resulted in the identification of 49 intermediate categories. The intermediate categories selected were broad enough to encompass the properties and dimensions of the initial concepts. The relationships and interaction between these categories also needed to be defined and characterised further. This process will be outlined in further detail in subsequent chapters.

The intermediate categories identified were as follows:

| | | | |
|---|---|---|---|
| Communication | Senior Management | Conflict Resolution | Monitoring |
| Language | Culture | Infrastructure | Skills Level |
| Knowledge Transfer | Mentoring | Cost | Fear |
| Documentation | Always Saying Yes | Team Building | Roles |

| | | | |
|---|---|---|---|
| Level of Contact | Coordination | Team Support | Trust |
| Hierarchy | Meetings | Distance | Partitioning |
| Staff Turnover | Training | Social Interaction | Structure |
| Effort | Gender | Experience | Teamness |
| Risk | Time Zone | Skills Database | Tools |
| Motivation | Public Holiday | Restrictions | Locations |
| Project Management | Cooperation | Vendor Support | |
| Lack of Support | Process | Over working | |
| Conflict | Configuration Management | Visibility | |

## 4.3 Selective Coding

The selective coding process is defined as the integration and refining of theory. It takes place over time and is the result of the researcher's immersion in the data. It comes from the identification of a core or central category. The function of the core category is to integrate the theory and render it dense and saturated which leads to a more theoretical completeness.[6]

Having defined the central category, the identification and development of explanatory concepts began. These provided the basis for the development of the key factors. The objective of this exercise was to outline the key variables and factors which the research had identified and which directly and indirectly facilitated or hindered effective virtual team software testing.

## 4.4 High-Level Categories

The intermediate categories were further refined by focusing on the central category which had been identified. This resulted in the broadening of some categories and the consolidation of others. These broader – (albeit fewer) - categories were somewhat of a distraction from the more original concepts and yet they were necessary in order to incorporate the properties and dimensions of all the concepts and categories they encapsulated.

---

[6] Strauss, A.L., Qualitative Analysis for Social Scientists 1987, Cambridge, UK: Cambridge University Press.

### 4.4.1 The Identification of High-Level Categories

The data, concepts and intermediate categories were reviewed and three high-level categories were identified along with the central category, fear. The three high level categories were:

- Culture
- Communication
- Project Management

The central category and the three high-level categories were broad enough to incorporate the other 45 intermediate categories as illustrated in Figure 4.2. These relationships and impacts are explored further in subsequent chapters.

Figure 4.2: Intermediate Categories Grouped Under and the Central High-Level Categories

## 4.6 Conclusion

In this chapter, the objectives and practicalities of undertaking a grounded theory-based strategy have been outlined. These included the details of the interview transcriptions and the focus groups' microanalysis processes. The preparation of memos and the use of open and axial coding which culminated in the identification of 49 intermediate categories was also presented. Following additional analysis, the central category - fear – and a further three high-level categories - communication, project management and culture - all emerged from the data. These high-level categories will be discussed in more detail in the subsequent chapters of this volume.

# CHAPTER FIVE

# CULTURE

## 5. Culture and its Impact on Virtual Teams

Recognising the importance and impact of "cultural distance" between remote colleagues plays a key role in the successful operation of virtual software teams. Culture can be defined as the: "*socially derived, taken for granted assumptions about how to act and think*". It remains "hidden beneath" our everyday consciousness and only becomes obvious when it is contrasted with different cultural norms, values and assumptions. The operation of virtual teams requires a level of cooperation and coordination that cannot ignore the impact which cultural distance plays and the barriers and misunderstandings which it can create.

Evidence emerged at an early stage of the participatory observational research that the management of the test operations were completely unaware of the implications of cultural distance and the impact it had on the day-to-day operation of their virtual teams. In addition to this, the Irish-based staff had a different experience because they previously collaborated with teams in other international locations and on a regular basis. After further investigation, it transpired that this collaboration had proved problematic as a result of the cultural differences which arose. While management acknowledged the existence of these problems at the time, steps were not taken to address them and the issue was generally ignored. This approach helped to explain why due consideration had not been given to cultural distance and its impact on the operation of the virtual teams when the virtual teams were first established.

At the most basic level, there was very little information shared regarding the national cultures of the virtual teams at both locations. One Irish-based team member did not even know where the Asian country was located. This was made clear when they stated with reference to the Asian country: "*it is just their Middle Eastern culture*". The same person went on to express their surprise that they were working with Asian team members who were of a different ethnic background:

> "Another thing, sometimes they are not necessarily all from [XXXXX . You could have [another Asian ethnic group]; I am working with [another Asian ethnic group]!"

Clearly, this individual was not even aware where this country was in Asia. Furthermore, they had not been informed that this particular country's population was made up of three different Asian ethnic groups, this despite the fact that this Irish person had been part of a virtual team for a period of six months. Therefore, it was not surprising to find that the Irish-based virtual team members knew very little about the culture of their Asian colleagues. It was also clear from the focus group discussions that their Asian colleagues knew as little about Irish culture as the Irish-based staff did about Asian Culture.

Two relevant issues were highlighted here based on the analysis of the data. The first related to the approach taken to implement both virtual team strategies and the second was regarding how the teams operated as a result. The strategy in both situations was simply to replicate the procedures and processes implemented with the help of co-site teams. This "issue" manifested itself in a number of ways which included the lack of provision for basic cultural training and the non-addressing of related communication problems. Other issues which were highlighted included the problem of not recognising the need to inform each location regarding the other's national holidays. In addition, staff were not informed about the introduction of summer daylight-saving time and the impact that this would have on the amount of time both locations had for synchronous collaboration.

## 5.1 Cultural Problems: The Teams' Historical Perspective

The Irish-based virtual team members had previously worked on projects with colleagues located in Asia, North America and the Middle East, albeit, not as part of virtual teams. An unexpected outcome of the data analysis was that the Irish staff experienced most of their cultural problems when working with their colleagues located in the Middle East. As a result of additional research, it emerged that the root cause of these problems was from a lack of information and a lack of understanding with regard to the predominant cultures of both locations. Staff were not informed of what was culturally acceptable or unacceptable behaviour.

This resulted in situations where national cultural norms and styles of communication were employed which were misinterpreted. Unfortunately, this had a negative impact on communication, cooperation and the level of working relationships which existed between remote colleagues at both locations.

To place the cultural problems which were experienced here in context, it is of interest to note that this Middle Eastern country had been ranked in fifty-second position out of fifty countries and three regions based on the power-distance index. The concept of power-distance is defined as follows: "The extent to which people accept that power is distributed unequally". This term has also been described as "revering hierarchy". The ranking this Middle Eastern country received indicated that - as a country - they have a very low score for revering hierarchy. This was reflected in the fact that some individuals had a very blunt or "forthright" communication style. While such a style can be advantageous in certain situations, it can also be misinterpreted as aggressive or confrontational behaviour when dealing with other cultures.

Interestingly, the Irish had a very similar attitude to hierarchy and Ireland was ranked forty-ninth in the power index. Where the Irish and the workers from this Middle Eastern country differed was in how that attitude was communicated. Irish people are generally polite, friendly and helpful in their professional relationships with others.[1] This approach conceals the fact that - with Irish people generally - respect has to be earned and is not necessarily ascribed to a specific job title, role or position. People are judged on what they do and how they do it. In a cultural sense therefore, the Irish can be described as achievement-based in their outlook.[2] The Irish attitude towards authority is reflected in their humour toward themselves, their colleagues and their superiors. In these circumstances it is not surprising that - given the different cultural approaches to communication which both groups employed – there were some misunderstandings and expressions of hostility.

The experience of Irish-based staff when dealing with their Middle Eastern colleagues can be summed up in the following two statements:

---

[1] Gunnigle, P., N. Heraty, and M. Morley, Doing Business in.. The Republic of Ireland. Thunderbird International Business Review, 2002. 44, (5): p. 649 - 674.

[2] Trompenaars, F. and C.M. Hampden-Turner, Riding the Waves of Culture: Understanding Cultural Diversity in Global Business 2nd ed. 1998, New York, NY, USA: McGraw-Hill.

> "I worked with [a Middle Eastern country] before this and [people there] were very hard to deal with. They were arrogant and they could not take criticism. It was - if you logged a PR [Problem Report]- it was like if you were insulting them. [The attitude was] 'You could not find a problem in my piece of code'."

> "We would have experienced some rude comments and alienation from the team in [the Middle Eastern country] as such it is a cultural thing."

The latter part of this statement - made by a Project Manager - summed up the "reality" of the situation. Although it was realised at a managerial level that there was a cultural problem, no measures were taken to address it. Therefore, on both sides there was very little understanding of the perspective of their respective remote colleagues. As one respondent stated:

> "We did not absolutely know anything about their culture. We did not know it or understand it. We did not know if they were just being [Middle Eastern] or just being aggressive."

The Irish-based staff realised that cultural training was needed and if it had been provided a lot of problems could have been avoided. One respondent's evaluation of their Middle Eastern colleagues was as follows:

> "I am also conscious of the fact that two of the [Middle Eastern people] that I worked with came over to Ireland and they were lovely people. It was that they were just quite gruff. They were quite straight to the point and it took me weeks to realise that."

Regardless of the previous negative experience of the Irish-based staff and management in dealing with culturally-remote colleagues, the need for cultural training was not identified at a managerial level. This had particular relevance when the virtual team strategy was implemented with staff in the Middle Eastern country.

## 5.2 National Public Holidays

As identified in the early stages of the participant observational research, the lack of information on national public holidays between sites had been an area that warranted further investigation. During the interview phase, this issue was discussed with each of the interviewees. As a result, it became apparent that the majority of the Irish-based staff were not informed when their remote colleagues were celebrating national holidays. Equally there was no procedure in place to inform the Far Eastern team members of Irish national holidays. This lack of information had repercussions for the operation of the teams. When people are aware that their remote colleagues are going to be out of the office, they may raise urgent issues at an earlier time. In other situations, they may defer dealing with a matter that requires prompt input from the other location until they know the person is available to deal with the issue. Contacting remote colleagues on an urgent matter and hearing nothing back is a frustrating and de-motivating experience.

An interesting aspect of this issue was highlighted when a Project Manager stated that - as far as they knew - their Irish-based staff were informed when Far Eastern national holidays were taking place. When some of the Irish-based members of this Manager's team were questioned on this matter they made it clear that - in the majority of situations - they were not informed. Two representative responses are provided here:

> "I am not told if the [Far Eastern] team members are having a national holiday".

> "The [Far Eastern] team members have a lot of bank holidays. It would be handy to know when they are."

Another Project Manager stated that their remote team members were informed of Irish national holidays. When interviewing a member of that Manager's team it became clear that this was not the case as a conference call had been organised for the $17^{th}$ of March (St Patrick's Day, a public holiday in Ireland). The respondent stated that:

> "I actually had to send out a cancellation. We were supposed to have a conference call tomorrow, the $17^{th}$ of March. I just sent out a cancellation, but I nearly forgot to. They could very easily have been turning up."

## 5.3 Knowledge of the Culture of Remote Colleagues

A knowledge of the national culture and values of virtual team members is important in helping individuals interpret and understand the behaviour of their remote and culturally-diverse colleagues. The ability to classify culture allows it to be contrasted, compared, evaluated and predicted.

It was noted that Karolak's three points of cultural difference for interacting with and managing remote staff were incorporated in the different approaches outlined:

1. Some cultures do not promote individual responsibility and accountability.
2. Some cultures accept most suggestions without much discussion.
3. If things appear to be too good to be true, they probably are.

Hofstede's five dimensions, Trompenaars and Hampden-Turner's seven dimensions and Hall's seven concepts of culture were considered of value and utilised to sensitise the researcher's focus. The data which emerged during the preliminary results of the observational research highlighted the relevance of these issues.

## 5.4 Cultural Difference

The remotely-based team members come from a Far Eastern culture and this was reflected in their day-to-day activities as virtual team members. This contrasted sharply with the culture of the Irish team members i.e. which is Western in focus. When asked about their Far Eastern colleagues, the Irish-based staff generally described them as respectful, friendly, polite and hardworking. However, they went on to state that clear work-related differences existed between the Irish and Far Eastern based staff.

### 5.4.1 Gender

Computing World is a worldwide equal opportunity employer and does not allow gender bias in its recruitment or its internal promotion policies. This was represented in the gender mix of the Irish-based staff where two of the virtual team Project Managers were female. At a professional level, gender was not an issue and was not even considered relevant within the Irish division.

This is not the case in some Eastern cultures, however, cultures where the female role can be viewed as subservient to that of the male. In these societies a woman's principal responsibility after marriage is primarily that of nurturer and homemaker. In such cultures, attitudes to gender which are considered totally unacceptable by Western standards, are still prevalent and accepted as the norm. This may be reflected in such customs as women being legally required to cover their heads in public, receive limited/or no education, having to obey their fathers, accept arranged marriages or having to obey their husbands in all matters. This attitude to women is sometimes reinforced by certain religious beliefs and

– in some countries - by the legal system. Even in a progressive country, such as the Far Eastern country in question here, women were always subject to religious law with respect to all family and religious matters.

When establishing the Far Eastern operation, Computing World employed its equal opportunity strategy and a mixed gender work force was recruited. In general, the Far Eastern country, which is predominantly a Muslim country, is perceived as a progressive, industrialised, and outward-looking society. The fact that it has two other significant religious and ethnic minorities has necessitated the need for the establishment of what is perceived as an "open" and "inclusive" society. That said, a large percentage of the population continue to hold - what in the Western world – might be considered conservative and/or traditional beliefs.

With specific regard to gender, a respondent who visited the Far Eastern office outlined his experience as follows:

> "The women, they all wore scarves, the long scarf over their heads. Well not all of them, but most of them. They are quite religious and devout."

Regarding working on-site with Far Eastern based female colleagues, he outlined his experience as follows:

> "There were no problems with the women working, but although, as I said, the women were very quiet and reserved. They did not like to ask questions or to say they did not understand, or look for clarification of something."

The initial analysis of the data did not identify any specific problems regarding gender-related virtual team interaction. During the on-site aspect of the investigation the Far Eastern males did not demonstrate any reluctance reporting to and working with Irish-based female Project Managers, Team Leaders and Engineers. The Irish-based team members were not aware of offending the sensibilities of their male or female Far Eastern based colleagues. That said, as one respondent pointed out:

> "Given that we have no idea about their culture we would not know if we had offended them or not. It is not like they would tell you [sic]".

While problems in this area did not emerge during the on-site aspect of this investigation, they did occur later. A Project Manager outlined her experience on visiting the Far Eastern country and meeting a new Far Eastern Manager who was working on her project. On meeting him, she offered to shake his hand, but he refused to do. In fact, he put his hands behind his back. She went on to state that she found him uncooperative in general. As a result of his attitude, she had to change her management style in her dealings with him. Rather then employing her normal approach of discussing matters and gaining a consensus on how issues should be addressed, she had to dictate her instructions and insist that they were carried out to the letter. After a short period of time this Far Eastern based Manager was removed from the project. Having enquired as to the reason for his behaviour, she was told that he held strong religious beliefs and that he did not like reporting to a woman. She went on to say this made sense to her - since the possibility of gender-related issues arising with her virtual team had been discussed with the researcher during the on-site aspect of this investigation.

### 5.4.2 Religion

In the cultural and organisational setting, Hofstede outlines religion as one of the three factors of uncertainty avoidance. Religion is societal in nature and has a direct impact on the values, norms and morality of the individuals who adhere to a particular belief system. In societies where one religion dominates, its beliefs and norms tend to be socialised to the wider community and, to a limited extent, they become societal norms. In a global context, these societal norms are not necessarily understood or appreciated by people from another culture. Indeed, what in some cultures are considered acceptable practises and beliefs are considered unacceptable and, on occasions, offensive in others. In the organisational and (particularly) virtual team settings, a basic appreciation of remote colleagues' religious beliefs and practices, particularly which impact directly on the working environment, is very valuable.

With reference to the virtual teams researched, no such information or training was provided to staff at either location.

> "Islam is the predominant religion in "the Far Eastern country" and exerts a great influence not only on the methods of worship, but [that country's] way of life"

For the Irish perspective on religion this can be contrasted with a respondent's statement:

> "Everyone knows, we are all Irish Catholics here in Ireland."

While the universalism of that statement is not technically correct, Ireland has a predominantly Christian culture. Religious differences do arise with regard to attitudes in the areas of morality, gender, alcohol, diet, social interaction and daily prayer. With regard to asking visiting Far Eastern team members to attend informal social events, one respondent stated that:

> "Given the need for a social aspect when they were over they were invited out, but they did not turn up. Depends what they thought if we were going to pubs. I don't know. Can they drink? They might not be happy in a pub."

One respondent who visited the Far Eastern office was surprised to discover that they had a prayer space which was used by some staff for daily prayer during working hours:

> "One day I was walking past an office area and I saw this guy I wanted to speak to. I looked over the cubicle and asked him a certain question. I then only realised, looking at the room itself that it was a prayer room".

In this situation a basic knowledge and respect for each other's religious beliefs would have been of value and would have helped to develop some level of understanding between remote colleagues.

### 5.4.3 Power Distance

A clear picture of the Far Eastern team members' attitude to authority emerged from the data. One respondent who travelled to the Far Eastern country to provide training stated:

> "hierarchy is important to them. Most of them would have done what I said regardless if they thought it was right or wrong. I could have told them black was white and some people would have questioned it, more would have just done it."

This unquestioning attitude to authority had serious implications. It manifested itself in agreeing with everything that was said and saying "yes" to every management request. On the Far Eastern side there was a clear reluctance to express an opinion – i.e. to disagree or say what they really thought.

The Project Manager of team 'Alpha' who had been working with Far Eastern virtual team members for over a year-and-a-half realised that this unquestioning behaviour was a response to the managerial position that he held. This attitude was something which he and his colleagues had not experienced before as outlined here:

> "I view my position as a role, rather then a position. Where as they started doing what I was asking without questioning it and I actually did not like that… again once we got the point across to the [Far Eastern] Manager: 'Lads we are peers here we have got to work together I want to hear your team suggestions', but it took a while".

The Far Eastern team members were not familiar with this style of management.

In the IBM questionnaire on which his research was based Hofstede asked the question: "*How frequently in your experience does the following problem occur: Employees being afraid to express disagreement with their managers*?" He went on to state: "*Of all the questions in the questionnaire this one most clearly expresses power distance*". Power distance clearly was a relevant issue when working with the Far Eastern virtual team members. The Project Manager went on to outline the measures taken to overcome these problems: "*We got that gradually out of their systems, because it took us a long time to.*" It was only after being repeatedly told that it was acceptable - and (indeed) expected - that they be forthright and say what they really thought, that the Far Eastern team members were able to express their opinions to the Project Manager.

While the steps outlined had been taken to address these problems they had not been fully resolved. The Project Manager went on to state:

> "I think [The Far Eastern Manager] is a different type of manager… He finds it hard to get the information out of his own engineers. He eventually gets it out of them that this is wrong and then he will highlight it to me… They are a bit nervous maybe about that, of highlighting things to me, but we drag it out of them."

The Far Eastern Manager continued to find it difficult to get his own staff to tell him what they really thought or even that they were having problems.

The Far Eastern virtual team members also demonstrated another aspect of the power distance dimension. This was the fact that instructions must be conveyed by the correct authority figure – the person to whom obedience is expected. This was highlighted by the experience of an Irish-based Senior Tester who was asked by his Project Manager to pass on instructions to his Far Eastern colleagues with regard to the automation of specific test cases. His request was ignored, however as he stated: "*They would rather hear it from the boss than from me before they do anything.*"

The Senior Tester was perceived by his Far Eastern peers as not having the authority to make such a request although he had made it clear that he was acting on the Project Managers' instructions. Rather than challenge the Senior Tester on his authority to make the request, the Far Eastern team members just chose to ignore it. In this way confrontation was avoided.

### 5.4.4 The Implications of Saying "Yes"

The initial impact of the Far Eastern staff not saying "no" was that they ended up being seriously overworked. When requests were made for work to be undertaken within tight deadlines, their answer was always - "*yes we can do it*". As Hofstede pointed out when discussing individualism versus collectivism - in a collectivist culture, the maintenance of harmony within the organisation is considered a virtue and confrontation is generally avoided. In these circumstances saying "no" is considered confrontational. Similarly, saying "yes" does not indicate acceptance or approval. It can simply be a means of keeping the channels for communication open.

The Far Eastern staff carried out the extra work and completed it on time. Rather than confronting their Irish-based Managers and Team Leaders and saying "no" to requests, they said "yes" to everything and worked excessive hours of unpaid overtime as a result. While this level of effort was sustainable in the short term, in the longer term it became intolerable. When they could no longer endure these long hours, they left the organisation. This resulted in a high level of labour turnover in the Far Eastern country. Initially, the Irish-based management were not aware why this was happening. Once it became clear what was going on, the Test Manager gave clear instructions that remote staff were not to be asked to take on excessive amounts of work.

The Irish-based test operation management realised that overworking remote staff was an unacceptable and unproductive practice. Experienced engineers who had been trained in their specific roles were being forced to leave the organisation. It was realised that this was an expensive and inefficient strategy, given the time, cost and effort involved in recruiting and training technically-competent engineers.

### 5.4.5 Cultural Difference: Use or Misuse?

While it was determined by the Irish-based management of the test operation that requesting remote staff to work excessive hours was counterproductive, this was not a universally-held belief. Another division within the corporation had a different approach: When the management of that division realised that the Far Eastern staff did not refuse extra work and were prepared to work long hours, this was perceived as an opportunity that could be leveraged. The experience of a Project Manager who had a dual reporting role – i.e. reporting to both the Irish-based test operation and this other division - is summarised as follows:

> "In [the other division] I had an attitude problem according to them because I did not believe in the 7/12 attitude (working staff 12 hours a day, 7 days a week) and they were, like [sic] 'Why are your guys not working 50 hour weeks?' and I was like [sic], saying 'that is stupid and I am not going to do that'... I was hit by that type of attitude by very senior people."

When the interviewer asked whether the other managers in that division would have their staff work such long hours, the respondent replied:

> "Well, people will do it. One of my peers has his development organisation working 12 hours a day, 7 days a week, but he has huge attrition [labour turnover]."

They went on to say concerning their own Far Eastern team members:

> "It does not matter how good the work environment is, people will move for money as well. I have an element of attrition; I don't have it as bad. If I had listened to the supposed advice I was getting from my Senior Managers I would be in a much worse position."

The respondent believed that the outcome of not implementing a 7/12 strategy was successful in the long run.

> "I came out of it better. The [Far Eastern] team members have quoted my name personally as someone who stabilized [the project]."

She went on to state:

> "My approach is not encouraged (in the other division) this is what I am saying in a global environment it is like [sic] they are over in the [Far Eastern country]; they are happy to work those hours, so let them do it."

The Project Manager's decision to take a long-term approach led to the establishment of a more "stable" team. Indeed, where other Far Eastern teams had a very high staff turnover, people wanted to join this particular Project Manager's team. This came at a cost however; the Project

Manager initially felt alienated from her peers: *"I did not make friends initially because I did not comply with what they wanted"*. She also felt her achievements were still not fully appreciated by Senior Management in the other division.

> "The disconnect between the senior management support I got in [the other division] was my biggest disappointment and only because of [The Test Manager], I did not suffer at the end of year. I have the respect of people around me and that is more important."

This illustrates a very important lesson with regard to virtual team operation and distributed software development with reference to culture: *"If things appear to be too good to be true, they probably are"*. Without understanding the culture of the staff at the remote location, a factor that may appear as something that can be leveraged can, in fact, end up being totally counterproductive. The short-term impact of implementing a 7/12 strategy was increased productivity; the long-term implications were more serious, as a high level of staff turnover led to a loss of specific technical experience and competence. This was reflected in the limited long-term productivity levels which could be achieved as a result.

The management of the test operation did not wish to incur high-level labour turnover as they considered it uneconomic and a waste of resources. This view may not have been one that was universally held within the corporation, however. An important factor is always the cost element which is involved. It can be considered by some organisations and divisions a worthwhile exercise to achieve short-term productivity at the expense of hiring and retraining staff - particularly given the low wage costs in remote locations. This is particularly relevant if an organisation or division is at what is termed *stage three* – i.e. the 'cost strategy' stage of the Offshore Stage Model [94, 134]. At that stage in an organisation's outsourcing/offshoring strategy, the focus is purely on cost-saving.

It is worth noting that - if this was the situation - it should really have been communicated as an overall objective to the relevant Project Manager. While the manager was criticised for not implementing the relevant approach, she was not informed that the implementation of such a strategy was a divisional objective. In these circumstances the question remains: was it a short-sighted cost-saving exercise or a divisional strategy to leverage the availability of a large high skilled labour pool in a low cost location? Clearly, in the Project Manager's view, and given her reluctance to implement it, it was the former rather the later.

## 5.5 The Need for Cultural Training

This research demonstrated the need for appropriate cultural training and the negative impact of not providing cultural training for both the Irish and Far Eastern virtual team members. This reality was voiced by the respondents themselves: *"Some training on culture would be helpful"*. Given the lack of clear information regarding each other's culture, it was easy to understand how and why actions and issues were misinterpreted and led to misunderstandings. A respondent outlined his experience with a Far Eastern colleague whom he had been joking with as follows:

> "I actually had a situation last week where I had to tell this guy to remove his witticism from his strategy document Ha, Ha. He was trying to emulate the jocose Irish mentality I think."

The Far Eastern colleague did not realise that placing a joke in a strategy document was inappropriate behaviour. Whilst his Irish colleague found it amusing and understood why it had happened, he still found it unacceptable:

> "Ya. Because it is strange to find …He transferred this humour into the document. I was like: no, no not there anywhere, but there. You can send it to me in a mail, you can phone me, but not in a document."

There was equal potential for cultural problems to arise on the Irish side. This was exemplified by the experience of an Irish-based virtual team member who mentored a Far Eastern woman who travelled to Ireland for training. The Far Eastern woman wanted to know every single thing which the Mentor did. She also insisted on re-running a number of test cases which the Mentor had already passed. The Mentor's reaction was: *"I felt like she was checking up on me. She did not realise she was kind of insulting me"*. The outcome of such an approach could have been very serious as indicated by the Mentor: *"I admit it I did... when she would ask me a question I would get very defensive"*. It was pointed out that this woman came from a culture where it was important to correctly follow each process to the letter. In these circumstances, it was more than likely that she re-ran the test cases to be sure that she understood what she had been shown. The Mentor said that she did not realise this since she knew nothing about the girl's culture.

The Mentor then went on to say:

> "She asked me some personal questions. My religion and that sort of stuff - but I would never ask her that because I don't know what her culture will accept".

The question regarding her religion was considered totally unacceptable by the Mentor. Such questions only further compounded the difficulties experienced between the two individuals. Although, - in an Irish context - this was a totally inappropriate question to ask clearly the trainee did not realise that she was offending the Mentor. Both individuals had not received any training in each other's culture and as a result there was a direct breakdown in their working relationship. When discussing the implications of this experience, the Mentor stated: *"Yes it is important to understand other people's culture"*. In these circumstances, the need for staff at both locations to receive cultural training was vital. It is important to stress that discussion of cultural training is itself a sensitive subject and runs a danger of the reinforcement of out-of-date or "wooden" stereotypes. Cultures are made up of individuals, all of whom are not the same. There are common characteristics that distinguish one culture from another. Therefore, there are general activities, issues and approaches that need to be recognised. There are also certain activities and types of behaviour which are acceptable in one culture but which are unacceptable in another, and this fact needs to be appreciated.

> "One must understand other people in the context of their unique history, political, economic, social and cultural backgrounds. In that way it is possible to become more effective interactors with them".

This approach provides the basis and is a good starting point. Building on this basic knowledge and getting to know remote colleagues in order to lever their experience is the most effective way of developing a meaningful understanding of each other's culture.

In response to the question on the questionnaire: "*Would training in [Far Eastern] culture help?",* nine out of the ten respondents affirmed that it would. As outlined, it emerged from the interviews and focus group sessions that the Irish team members had little or no knowledge about their remote colleagues' culture. When it was discussed, they recognised the importance which culture played in the day-to-day activities of their respective virtual teams, and as a consequence, they expressed a clear desire to find out more about it. There was certainly an element of reticence regarding communicating and cooperating with their Far Eastern colleagues. That said, the Irish staff did not want to say or do anything that might be considered offensive or rude to their Far Eastern colleagues. One focus group participant summed this up when he stated: "*I want to know what I should not say or do; I don't want to insult anyone*".

### 5.5.1 Cultural Profiles

Two distinctive and very different cultural profiles emerged from the data analysis with respect to the Irish team members and the Far Eastern-based team members.

**The Irish-Based Staff**

The Irish-based staff were normally friendly, polite and helpful. They were not afraid to express themselves and generally told their managers what they thought. This was not presented in an aggressive or confrontational manner. In normal circumstances, through frank and meaningful exchanges between Engineers, Team Leaders and Managers, an agreement was reached. This approach to achieving consensus was expected and encouraged. Respect for authority had to be earned and was not ascribed to any individual, purely based on their role within the organisation. This fact was specifically highlighted by the Test Manager.

The Irish-based staff did not experience any problems in saying "no" to requests that they could not complete within their normal working day. As an Irish-based Team Leader stated: *"I am saying to Irish people: this is really important. Can you get this done as soon as possible? They will say: no. I can't do this until tomorrow".* The majority of Irish staff worked the standard working hours and would only consider working unpaid overtime in exceptional circumstances. In an Irish context gender was not an issue; males and females were regarded as peers and treated accordingly.

The use of humour is an important element in the Irish cultural profile. It is used in a friendly manner, although it can, on occasions, contain elements of sarcasm. It is very rarely intended to offend, but its directness can sometimes be misunderstood. In Ireland, generally, and in the organisation researched here, religion is considered a personal matter and does not impact on the working environment.

**The Far Eastern-Based Staff**

The Far Eastern-based staff were described as friendly, polite, courteous and hardworking. Given their high regard for hierarchy, they showed respect to their managers by agreeing with them. They were not inclined to express personal opinions and found it difficult to do so, even when pressed on a particular issue. They regularly worked long hours after their "official" finishing time. When asked to do something by a person in authority they immediately said "yes", considering it impolite to say "no". When such long hours became intolerable - rather than refusing to do these long hours - they simply left the organisation for another position elsewhere.

An important aspect of their respect for hierarchy was that, in order to comply with their instructions, they felt that these instructions had to come from the correct person, i.e. the person with the appropriate authority to make such a request. Confrontation was avoided at all costs. They appeared to be devout and religious people. When visiting Ireland for training they did not socialise with the Irish-based staff and declined invitations to informal social activities. They showed a preference for socialising within their own group. While different attitudes to gender existed between the Far Eastern- and Irish-based staff this did not initially impact on their professional activities. It did emerge at a later stage however and a Far Eastern Manager was actually removed from one of the projects due to his attitude in this regard.

## 5.6 Culture and Fear

A lack of knowledge regarding the culture of remote colleagues can directly lead to misunderstandings and this can add to the level of fear and mistrust which is experienced when operating a virtual team. In this investigation - and given the level of fear experienced by the Irish-based virtual team members - it was not surprising that cultural differences added to the overall level of concern. This was highlighted by the Far Eastern virtual team members' willingness to work excessively long hours, a fact which contrasted sharply with the attitude of their Irish-based colleagues. The Irish had no problem saying they were unable to undertake extra work and normally did not work additional unpaid hours. This situation was highlighted in observations that emerged from within the virtual teams themselves. On a number of occasions, the Irish-based Team Leaders compared the 'positive' attitude of their Far Eastern-based team members with the more "robust" attitude of the Irish staff and this was articulated to the Irish team members on more then one occasion.

In addition to this, very little information or feedback was provided by the Far Eastern team members. In these circumstances - and without an adequate knowledge of the Far Eastern team members' culture - it was not unreasonable for the Irish staff to suspect that they were actively being "undermined" by their remote colleagues. The willingness of the Far Eastern workers to work intolerable hours the fact that they were two-fifths the "cost" (salary-wise) of an Irish-based team member - (a fact which corporate management continued to reiterate to the Irish-based staff) - only added to these suspicions. In these circumstances, it was not an unreasonable assumption for the Irish staff to suspect that their Far Eastern colleagues were actively trying to "take" the Irish team members' jobs. As one respondent stated:

> "Would they be actively trying to undermine us? I would not say they would be actively saying they were doing it."

## 5.7 Conclusion

In this chapter, the necessity of addressing cultural distance between virtual team members has been highlighted. A significant factor to emerge from this research was the difficulty which a lack of cultural awareness has on the operation of the virtual teams. It was clear the negative impact of cultural distance between the virtual team members had not been recognised by management. This lack of communication also took place in a context where the Project Managers and Irish-based team members had previously had negative experiences when dealing with colleagues from different cultures. Indeed, negative attitudes were still prevalent towards former remote colleagues when cultural issues were discussed during the course of this research project.

Having analysed the data with reference to the intermediate categories and the high-level category culture, the importance and implications of this key factor emerged. These findings were reviewed with relevance to the results from the analysis of the data. This helped to contextualize the cultural experiences of the Irish-based virtual team members with those of their remote colleagues, and the full implications of cultural distance. This culminated in the identification of the impact of culture on these key factors - coordination, cooperation, knowledge transfer, project management, communication and risk (see Figure 5.1).

The reverence for hierarchy had serious repercussions on the level of labour turnover amongst the Far Eastern team members. This had potentially significant implications too for the successful project management of the virtual teams since it directly increased the levels of risk involved. It also had specific repercussions for coordination since there was a positive response to all requests but very limited feedback. In addition, knowledge transfer and training were both impacted upon since questions were not asked and there was no strategy in place for determining how successful these activities had been.

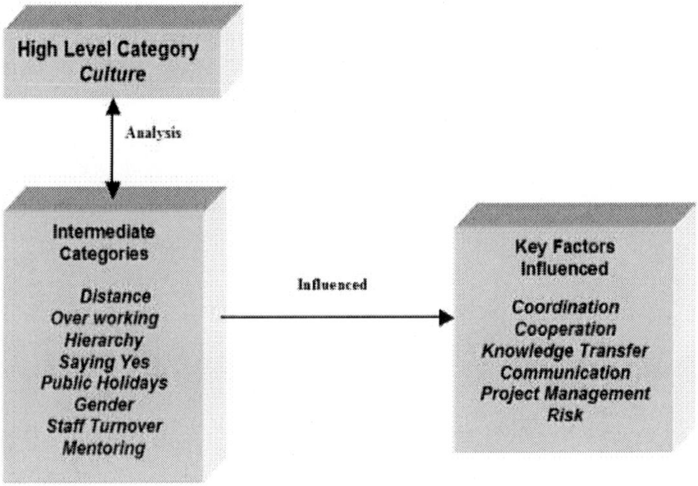


Figure 5.1: The Analysis of the High-Level Category Culture

The Irish-based virtual team members identified the need for cultural training so as to facilitate effective working relationships with their remote colleagues. The lack of the provision for cultural training between locations had direct implications for cooperation, coordination project management and communication. Lack of cultural training also added to the level of fear experienced by the Irish-based team members, since it appeared to them that their Far Eastern team members were trying to "take" their jobs – by working excessively long hours.

The Far Eastern team members cultural reluctance to refuse to take on additional work was eventually recognised as a problem by the test operation and steps were taken to prevent the Far Eastern staff working long hours. A separate division within the corporate organisation had a differing perspective regarding this cultural phenomenon and saw it as an opportunity that could be leveraged for its short-term advantage, regardless of its long-term implications. If the rationale for implementing such an approach was an overall cost saving strategy, this was not communicated to the relevant Project Manager.

# CHAPTER SIX

# COMMUNICATION

## 6. Communication and its Impact for Virtual Teams

The benefits and problems associated with communication in the virtual teams researched were clearly discernable in the data analysed. Its effects were far-reaching and impacted directly on the all aspects of the operation of the virtual teams. It was also evident that a number of the intermediate categories directly related to and impacted on communication.

A respondent outlined the specific communication-related differences they observed between being a member of a collocated and virtual team as follows:

> "[In the collocated team] you can just ask a question about a certain PR [problem report] or thing that happened. It takes two minutes and it is finished".

They also highlighted the benefits of being able to develop professional, face-to-face working relationships and the ease of sharing information with collocated colleagues. The loss of informal contact between remote team members has been identified as a specific problem for effective communication with distributed software development.[1]

Research carried out in the area of collocated software development found that, on average, seventy-five minutes a day was spent in unplanned interpersonal interactions.[2]

---

[1] Herbsleb, J.D., D.J. Paulish, and M. Bass. Global software development at siemens: experience from nine projects in Proceedings of the 27th international conference on Software engineering. 2005. St. Louis, MO, USA ACM.
[2] Perry, D.E., N.A. Staudenmayer, and L.G. Votta, People, organizations, and process improvement. IEEE Software, 1994. 11(4): p. 36 - 45.

The opportunity for this type of informal communication is seriously constrained by the implementation of a globally distributed software development strategy.[3] It has also been recognized that the absence or limited availability of nonverbal cues and gestures (context) makes it more difficult to achieve a shared understanding between remote team members.[4] As a respondent stated:

> "Because when they are here you don't have time zone problems, it is a lot easier to talk to people face to face".

The respondent then went on to articulate the communication problems they experienced working as a virtual team member:

> "The [Far Eastern team members] are eight hours ahead. A lot of the time when you raise a query you have to wait until the following day for a response."

The difficulties associated with organising virtual meetings with remote colleagues, given the temporal distance between sites, was also highlighted, as was the Far Eastern team members' mixed level of competency in their use and comprehension of English.

## 6.1 The Opportunity to Communicate

To enable effective cross-site communication, there needs to be the opportunity for such activity to occur. The most effective form of communication is synchronous in nature. Temporal difference directly impacts on the opportunity for such communication to take place.

### 6.1.1 Temporal Difference and National Holidays

Ireland, like the rest of the European Union, employs Daylight Saving Time (DST). This requires the time in all EU countries to go forward by one hour on the last Sunday in March and go back by the same period of time on the last Sunday in October. On Friday the last working day before the change to DST took place, having made numerous enquiries, the

---

[3] Handel, M. and J.D. Herbsleb. What is chat doing in the workplace? . in Proceedings of the 2002 ACM conference on Computer supported cooperative work 2002. New Orleans, Louisiana, USA.

[4] Kock, N., Benefits For Virtual Organizations From Distributed Groups Communications of the ACM 2000. 43(11): p. 107-112.

researcher was unable to determine what the implications of DST would be for the operation of the virtual teams.

Realising the importance of this issue he decided to implement an action research approach. The first step to diagnose the problem was to determine what the actual situation was. It emerged from his investigation that DST is not employed in the Far Eastern country. As a result, there was an extra hour in which synchronous communication could take place between sites during the DST period. When he able to contact a Project Manager, he discussed the matter with them. He was told they was unaware of this and thanked him for highlighting this issue. The action taking outcome from that discussion was that the Project Manager took on the responsibility for passing this information on to the staff.

As part of the evaluation and lesson learning process, the results from this incident were discussed with the Test Manager as he had been out of the office when this matter arose. He was informed that the Test Manager was aware that the Far Eastern country did not employ DST. The researcher queried why no one had been assigned responsibility to inform the Project Managers and virtual team members of that fact. While the current situation was not serious - it meant everyone had an extra hour to work with the Far Eastern country - this would not be the case the following October when that hour was lost. This demonstrated that the full implications of effective virtual team operation were not fully appreciated. It was also relevant to note that a virtual testing team had been in operation with members in the Far Eastern country for over eighteen months, yet this issue had not been raised and clarified before this incident.

### 6.1.2 Time Zone Difference between Ireland and the Far Eastern country

The Far Eastern country where the remote virtual team members were located is eight hours ahead of Ireland during the winter time period. This translates to an official overlap in working hours between locations of one hour, or thirty minutes, depending on what time the Irish staff start work. During the DST period, the official overlap in working hours is two hours or one and a half hours, again depending on the starting time of the Irish-based team members. All year round, it was not unusual to find Far Eastern team members still working at 7.00 p.m. Far Eastern time or later. It was obvious that the Far Eastern team members consistently worked long hours. One Irish team member even believed their remote colleagues did shift work, as they had been there so late in the past.

### 6.1.3 National And Religious Holidays

The Irish and Far Eastern virtual team members were not notified of national or religious holidays in the other's location. This problem resulted in virtual teams not being aware in advance that their colleagues would be unavailable on specific dates. As a result, issues were raised and they were not responded to within the normal timeframe. In these circumstances it was left to the engineers to determine why this was happening. This issue was of particular relevance to teams working with the Far Eastern country given the ethnic and religious mix of the Far Eastern population.

### 6.1.4 Overlap in Working Hours

An important aspect of the temporal issue was highlighted when a Project Manager was asked about the official overlap in working hours between Ireland and the Far Eastern country (during the winter period). They stated: *"there is only one hour officially of a workday overlap between Ireland and the [Far Eastern country]"*. When a senior member of that Project Manager's team was asked the same question they stated: *"With the [Far Eastern country] we only now have technically half an hour overlap. Most of us here do not start until 9.30 a.m.*". This meant there was an official overlap in working hours between locations of thirty minutes in winter and one hour and thirty minutes in summer. It was noted, given the importance of the opportunity for synchronous communication to take place - that this very limited time period did not appear to have been considered important by the Irish management.

The hours worked by the Far Eastern team members unofficially extended the widow of opportunity in which synchronous communication could take place. A respondent stated:

> "We certainly see anything up to 11 o'clock in the morning. We see e-mails coming across from them. So that would be 8.00 p.m. [sic - 7.00 p.m.] their time".

Even in these circumstances there was still limited opportunity for synchronous communication, particularly during the winter time period.

As the respondents raised the issue, the impact of temporal difference was investigated with reference to the timing of cross-site meetings. Given that the Far Eastern team members had initially worked very long hours, it was of interest to determine if the time zone difference had been given due consideration when organising this type of meeting. When the issue was discussed with a respondent they stated:

> "The [Far Eastern] team members are very accommodating. If you said you wanted a meeting at 2.00 p.m. here, 10.00 p.m. their time they would be there. There is actually in fact a meeting at 10 o'clock at night over there and they ring from home. So you would, quite often, hear the kids screaming in the background".

Due to the nature of the specific project this team were working on, important issues had to be discussed directly with Irish-, Far Eastern- and US-based staff. This brought three time zones into play. This issue was discussed with the relevant Project Manager who stated:

> "Obviously when we are trying to organise meetings (with the Far East) we organise them for the morning. There is a conflict…Because we are now working with three different time zones…you cannot get a time that everyone is in the office. It is one of the most difficult things to address".

This highlighted a serious temporal issue – i.e. there was no convenient time for tripartite cross-site meetings to take place. The time difference between locations was as follows:

- The Far Eastern country is eight hours (seven in summer) ahead of Ireland.
- Ireland is six hours ahead of the relevant location in North America.
- North America is fourteen (thirteen in summer) hours behind the Far Eastern country.

The solution was to hold the meeting during the wintertime period at 2.00 p.m. GMT in Ireland which was 10.00 p.m. in the Far Eastern country time and 8.00 a.m. Central Standard Time (CST). While this was a compromise, it permanently inconvenienced the Far Eastern staff. The temporal impact of the requirement for cross site synchronous communication on the personal lives of IT professionals involved in GSD has been recognized as a problem. This issue had particular relevance, given the Far Eastern staff's record of not complaining when expected to work antisocial hours and then just leaving the organisation.

## 6.2 Language. The Ability to Communicate

English was the language used for the day-to-day operation of the virtual teams. In this situation, staff in both locations required proficiency in both spoken and written English. This was a prerequisite for effective communication to take place and the successful operation of the virtual teams. To fully appreciate the situation which emerged from the analysis of the data with regard to language, it was important to place the subject in context.

### 6.2.1 Hiberno-English

The official first language of Ireland, under the Irish constitution, is Gaeilge (Irish). While this is the official position, the reality of the situation is rather different. English is the first language of all, but a very small percentage of the Irish population. The English spoken in Ireland is a separate dialect called Hiberno-English. The differences between British English and Hiberno-English are slight. There are some minor differences in usage and ordering of words, but they both employ the same grammar and spelling.

### 6.2.2 The Far Eastern team members' Knowledge of English

The analysis of the data from this research indicated that the Far Eastern staff had a mixed level of competency in their fluency in English. When asked the question how the Irish-based staff rated their Far Eastern colleagues level of English the following statement sums up the views of the respondents: *"Depending. There seems to be a wide spectrum; you can have excellent and very bad.*" There were mixed levels of linguistic competency experienced when dealing with the Far Eastern virtual team members. It depended on whom a respondent was dealing with in the Far East as to how they rated their knowledge of English.

During the interviews and focus groups, more than one question was asked on this topic. The replies from the Project Managers and a Trainer give a broad overview of the situation. A Project Manager stated:

> "…anytime I would have said something in conference calls, we would have to confirm it … In some cases we do not know for sure if they understand it or not".

They went on to say regarding one of their staff:

> "[An Irish Trainer] did experience people not interacting or understanding her, when she was doing the training [sic] with [the staff in the Far Eastern country]".

A second Project Manager highlighted the Far Eastern team members mixed level of competency as: *"The men are bad; the women are brilliant"*. An Irish Trainer who provided training in The Far Eastern stated: *"Some have good English; some have medium to basic English"*. He went on to say the major disadvantage of the virtual team strategy was:

> "Communication problems between here (Ireland) and there (the Far Eastern country) and there (the Far Eastern country) and the States due to a lack of English, or a lower standard of English."

A prerequisite for the implementation of a successful virtual team strategy is proficiency in a common language between participating staff at all locations. English is the lingua franca of the business, scientific and the IT industry in the twenty-first century. Computing World was well established in the Far Eastern country in question and its Human Resources (HR) department there would have been well acquainted with the linguistic capabilities of the local population. It was surprising then, that staff were recruited who did not have the required fluency in English, although they did have the basic technical skills required.

Research was undertaken to determine if the problems associated with the Far Eastern virtual team members mixed level of competence in English was specific to the organisation or was a wider issue. It was determined that it was a national issue for the Far Eastern country concerned. When the issue was discussed with a Trainer and later a Project Manager, the researcher asked if they thought the provision of English classes would be of value for those with a basic knowledge. The Trainer replied: *"I would say so, a lot of people over there might want to."* The Project Manager stated:

> "I have not thought about English classes for Computing World people over there. It is not even something I would have thought of doing to be honest. I would have considered it would be outside our realm of responsibility or sphere of influence".

This was an interesting response this Project Manager had specifically identified the low level of competency in their knowledge of English as a problem among some of their Far Eastern team members.

The virtual Alpha team had been in operation for a year and a half. Over that period, the work was being carried out, but clearly it was impacted by the factors outlined in this investigation. The Far Eastern team members' way of dealing with their different levels of linguistic competency was to instigate the use of informal spokespersons, as a respondent stated: "*With [ the Far Eastern] team members I don't know if they are shy or what, but they have a couple of spokespersons*". While this was not an ideal method of operation, it did go in some way to address the linguistic difficulties which were encountered.

### 6.2.3 Accent

The Irish-based respondents identified the Far Eastern accent as an additional problem that directly impacted on their ability to comprehend some of the verbal communications they received from their remote colleagues. The following two statements summarise the respondents' views on this issue:

*"Mind you I struggle with some of their accents, as they are hard to understand."*

*"Then there is the whole accent thing and people shout when they are speaking; other people don't."*

This provided a relevant discussion topic for the focus groups. When the researcher raised the subject, he suggested that the Far Eastern team members might have had equal difficulty understanding the Irish accent. This was followed in both cases by a discussion where it emerged the participants had not anticipated that their accents could have been a problem. They just assumed as they spoke English, everything they said would be clearly understood. As a result of the discussions that took place, they realised how their regional accents could be equally difficult for their Far Eastern colleagues to comprehend.

### 6.2.4 The Need for Training on How to Communicate

The need for training on how to effectively communicate with remote colleagues was identified. Communicating with people whose first language was not English and who came from a different culture was not a straightforward task. It requires the provision of relevant information, thought and due consideration. It was mentioned that the Irish have a tendency to speak quickly and their accent made it even more difficult for their Far Eastern colleagues to comprehend what they were saying. The relevance of the statement "*If there is one general law of communication it is we never communicate as effectively as we think we do*" needed to be considered and appreciated.

When speaking and writing to remote colleagues there was a need to keep the content concise and to the point. The content had to be expressed clearly and in unambiguous terms. The use of colloquialisms and local expressions should be avoided at all costs. It was recognised that the Far Eastern team members also required training in how best to communicate with their Irish colleagues. An important point to emerge from the focus groups was that, when a person did not understand a statement or a communication they received from a remote colleague, they should ask for that statement to be repeated or for it to be clarified further. Respondents had no idea what was and was not acceptable when communicating with their Far Eastern colleagues. This included what the their Far Eastern colleagues might have considered as insulting or an inappropriate form of communication.[5]

The respondents were asked if they had received training in how best to communicate with remote colleagues. A typical reply was "*No, but yes we would like it*". The value of such training was acknowledged and noted by a Project Manager when the matter was discussed with them. The requirement for this type of training has been identified in other relevant research.[6] As had the fact that the level of interaction, trust, commitment and candour between virtual team members were all improved as a result of the provision of such training.[7]

## 6.3 The Tools to Communicate

The organisation provided a broad selection of tools for the virtual team members to communicate with their remote colleagues. They included

---

[5] Herbsleb, J.D., D.J. Paulish, and M. Bass. Global software development at siemens: experience from nine projects in Proceedings of the 27th international conference on Software engineering. 2005. St. Louis, MO, USA ACM.

[6] Gluesing, J., et al., eds. The Development of Global Virtual Teams. Virtual Teams that Work: Creating Conditions for Virtual Team Effectiveness, ed. C.B. Gibson and C.S. G. 2003, Jossey-Bass. : San Francisco, CA, USA. 353 - 380.

[7] Warkentin, M. and P.M. Beranek, Training to improve virtual team communication. Information Systems Journal, 1999. 9(4): p. 271-289.

telephone, voicemail, e-mail, instant messenger, conference calls, NetMeeting and team intranet sites. An important aspect regarding the provision of communication tools is that while it is very important to have effective tools in place and available for use, it is equally as important to ensure people are actually motivated to utilise them. Motivation and fear were key issues that directly negatively impacted on the Irish based staff's use of synchronous communication tools.

### 6.3.1 Telephone and Voicemail

The issue regarding the quality of the telephone lines between Ireland and the Far Eastern country warrants further discussion as it was raised by a number of respondents during the interviews and can be summarised by the following statement: *"The lines can also be a bit tricky - a lot of static on it or echo."* The need for an effective telecommunications infrastructure is a prerequisite for geographically distributed software development activities to take place efficiently.

An additional telephone-related issue suggested by a number of the Irish staff was that they believed the Far Eastern team members had restrictions placed on them making international telephone calls to their Irish colleagues, due to the cost involved. This was explored during a number of interviews. In answer to questions on this topic, the majority of replies are summarized in the following statement: *"I would say they could be restricted on the amount of international calls they can make to Ireland."*

When this issue was discussed with a Project Manager and a member of staff who visited the Far Eastern office, they responded as follows: The Project Manager stated:

> "I have not experienced it to be honest. I would not be surprised if there were. I got an e-mail from them the other day saying would we pay for a PC (Personal Computer) for them to do something... They seem to be very, very careful of cost associated with anything."

The respondent who visited the Far Eastern office stated:

> "Oh yes they are very much restricted over there. The place I was in you had to have an AT&T calling card otherwise you could not make an outside call... It is more difficult over there to contact even your team members [in Ireland]. There is a real focus on cost and trying to keep costs down".

The analysis of the data did not provide conclusive evidence that the Far Eastern based virtual team members were formally restricted from telephoning their Irish colleagues. Indeed the Test Manager, when questioned on this very point, stated there were no restrictions in place. He also expressed surprise to hear that people believed there were. Regardless of there being formal restrictions in place or not, the reality for a large number of Irish-based staff was, as a respondent stated: *"nobody [from the Far Eastern country] rings me.*

What the research demonstrated was that the Far Eastern management were very aware that their competitive advantage lay in cost. There was also the belief by some Irish staff that the Far Eastern management were trying to transfer their costs to the Ireland budget. This added to the level of mistrust which these individuals felt toward their Far Eastern colleagues and increased their fears for the future of their jobs.

When their staff travelled to Ireland it was in economy class.

> "I was supposed to go [the Far Eastern country] at the start of the year with another girl and we were flying business class. They all came over in economy class".

When the Far Eastern team members were in Ireland their expenses, including travel, were strictly controlled.

> "They [the Far Eastern team members visiting Ireland] had only a couple of cars between them all so they had to wait until everyone was ready to go together as they could not afford the bus."

The fact that a Far Eastern team member did not have direct access to a telephone was also highlighted. The effective control of cost is an important aspect of every business operation. Where it hinders or delays business-related communication it can be a false economy and this is particularly pertinent when operating in a virtual team environment.

### 6.3.2 E-mail

E-mail was the preferred method of communication between the majority of the Irish-based team members with their Far Eastern colleagues. Their preferences are summarised by the following quote: *"E-mail would be how I normally communicate with [The Far Eastern country].* The practical advantages of utilising e-mail as an everyday communication tool are summarised as follows:

> "I prefer e-mail where you can write down certain lines and number one, number two, and number three. They can come back and say my answer to number one is."

One of the disadvantages identified was:

> "I sometimes think it is difficult to get anything more then just the information across. It is difficult to get any good feeling across or anything like that, so it is effective to a point".

There was a disproportionate dependence on the use of e-mail. Some of the respondents realised that the Irish-based teams\ excessive reliance on e-mail was an inefficient approach and their views are represented by the following statement:

> "I think it is a problem. We rely too much on e-mail when we communicate with the [Far Eastern country] and we should be using the phone more and they should be using the phone more."

It was also recognised that e-mail was a necessary tool and at times the most appropriate method of communication, given the temporal differences between locations and the need for an effective asynchro;nous tool. The biggest disadvantage to its use was the delay in response time which resulted. This was recognised by the respondents, whose views can be summarised by this typical statement: *"A lot of the time when you raise a query you have to wait until the following day for a response."* This problem directly impacted on the operation of the teams researched due to their excessive dependence on e-mail as their primary tool for communication between sites.

### 6.3.3 Instant Messenger

Instant Messenger was used by some Irish-based virtual team members and not by others. It emerged that the Far Eastern team members frequently used Instant Messenger to communicate with each other. A respondent who visited the Far Eastern office noted: *"That is a big thing over there - they use instant messenger, they all use it."* The members of the Alpha team frequently used instant messenger. Indeed, three respondents from that team rated it as their most preferred communication tool and provided positive feedback which can be summarised by the following statement: *"I use Instant Messenger a lot. I know a lot of the team use it...it is very handy."* This directly contrasted with the Beta team's rating of instant messenger, where it was their least preferred communication tool and as a result it was rarely used by them. The following statement summarises their attitude and lack of use of the tool: *"No I have not used instant messenger"*.

The relevant Project Manager provided the reason why Instant Messenger had not been used on the Beta team:

> "We don't actually use Instant Messenger and actually it is something we should use…I have just had this discussion with someone in my team the other day who had just discovered instant messaging and said it would be great to talk to the team in [the Far Eastern country]."

It is of relevance to note that the Beta team had been in operation for over six months and they were not using instant messenger. The Alpha team, on the other hand, which had been in operation for a year and a half, was making extensive use of the tool. Clearly the information that Instant Messenger was such a popular communication tool was not available to be leveraged by the Project Manager and members of the Beta team. Indeed they only '*discovered*' the tool when a team member highlighted its potential benefits.

Both virtual teams researched were operating in what could best be described as difficult circumstances. The objectives of both Project Managers were to undertake their respective virtual team projects in the most professional manner possible. In both cases this had to be carried out without the provision of specific GSD and virtual team knowledge, training or support in how best this could be achieved. There was also limited, but relevant experience which had not been shared. The success achieved by both teams to that point was directly attributable to the professionalism and experience of both Project Managers. The difference between virtual and collocated team operations are considerable and communication is a key area that needs to be addressed specifically. While an extensive range of communication tools were provided by the organisation very little information or support on their use was made available to the virtual team members.

A further point to note regarding the use the Alpha team made of Instant Messenger was that their respondents expressed a lower preference for the use of the telephone than the respondents from the Beta team. It is also relevant to state that fear of their jobs being offshored to the Far Eastern country was expressed equally by the Alpha team and Beta team members. With the exception of one respondent, there was no mention of the use of

Instant Messenger for the development of personal relationships between the Alpha team members and their remote colleagues. Being text-based, it did allow a certain element of impersonal contact. Clearly in this instance the gender and the first name of the recipient were not issues to prevent communication taking place at this specific level.

An additional benefit provided to the users of Instant Messenger was that when they or their remote colleagues were online, their presence was highlighted by the tool. That was of particular value given the temporal differences between sites. Instant Messenger also offered the facility to display a sign saying '*I am busy* or *I am away from my desk*'.

### 6.3.4 Conference Calls / NetMeeting

Teleconferencing call facilities were provided to allow conference calls to take place between remote team members. Facilities for NetMeeting teleconferencing presentations were also provided. Two specific types of conference call took place: The first type was status conference calls, where information and reports were presented and discussed. The second type of conference call utilised NetMeeting and was used for training and knowledge transfer. This method of training was extensively utilised by both teams researched.

The status conference calls took place on a regular basis. As a Project Manager stated: *"I think it is critical to have conference calls... to make sure things are going OK and check up on them".* The problems associated with these calls were outlined as follows:

> "We have two regular phone conference calls. I kind of don't look forward to the Friday one again because of the language."

> "It is quite difficult with a conference call…you have five people in a room and you are struggling with the accents in the first place…it is difficult to recognise who is talking…someone says something and someone else says something"

The Far Eastern virtual team members' knowledge and use of English and their accents were highlighted as issues that directly impacted on the Irish participants during these conference calls. An additional fact was that a procedure was not in place on how these calls should be conducted. Participants did not identify themselves when they made their contributions. This directly added to the level of confusion experienced by remote participants. There was also the additional problem of bad telephone connections between locations.

It was surprising, given the problems experienced, that conference calls were selected as a primary mechanism for providing training and knowledge transfer. In these circumstances, it was not totally unexpected that this approach had had limited success. As one Trainer stated: "*Some people have given workshops using NetMeeting. It is hard to use conference calls and describe everything over the phone"*. Another Trainer, who had planned to provide training in the Far Eastern country, was unable to make the journey. As an alternative, they provided the training using conference calls and NetMeeting facilities.

Initially, when they were asked how the provision of their training went, they stated "*I found it very effective for giving training"*. They went on to clarify that statement by outlining some of the problems they subsequently experienced:

> "When I was giving the training and I asked: 'Any questions?', no questions [were asked]. One of the guys that came over here who [sic] I had given training to... He attended a meeting here where the same material was presented... The following day I was mailed and told he was completely lost. I went over to him... He said he did not understand it. So I brought up the slides and showed them to him and he said he had never seen them before...So I went through them again. One of the problems is they are quick to say 'Yes I understand' when they don't."

There are a number of questions which arise from this incident. Was this person's lack of understanding wholly due to their reluctance to ask questions and say yes all the time? As discussed earlier, these are relevant issues and had to have played a part. In addition, could this participant understand what the Trainer was saying during the NetMeeting presentation? A Trainer who provided face-to-face training in the Far Eastern office stated his experience as follows:

> "For some of them you have to put things more simply, or speak a bit slower, but in general I was trying to accommodate different people in different groups. To try and account for their level of English and level of understanding."

Clearly the NetMeeting participant did not understand the presentation; indeed he had no recollection of even seeing the slides. In these circumstances, how effective the NetMeeting based training had been for the other participants needed to be considered. Without visual contact or knowledge of the technical and linguistic capabilities of participants, it was very difficult for the Trainer to prepare material and assess how their presentation was received. The Trainers did not have access to information regarding the Far Eastern staff's technical and linguistic capabilities.

Another respondent who also gave training using NetMeeting stated:

> "On the phone, we have NetMeeting calls - or conference calls we call them – with [the Far Eastern country]. They tend to be a bit confusing. Where we are presenting material and we don't hear any feedback from them and we ask can you repeat that please. They say it is the phone line, it might be a polite way of saying 'We don't have a clue what you are saying'."

It is of interest to note that, given the experience of both these Trainers, the practice of using conference calls and NetMeeting as a method of knowledge transfer continued to be used. This may well have been because it was the only option possible given the geographical distance between sites. While that may have been the case, its effectiveness was clearly limited as a medium to facilitate knowledge transfer.

A number of Far Eastern based engineers had travelled to Ireland for training which had proved more successful. This face-to-face interaction with their Irish based colleagues had also led to the development of relationships, which improved communication between them and their Irish colleagues on their return to the Far Eastern country. This was reflected in the quality of subsequent conference calls which these individuals participated in. A respondent stated: *"We now have conference calls with the people who were over here and it has made it easier*".

### 6.3.4.1 The Rejection of NetMeeting for Training Purposes

The analysis of the data generated from this investigation identified NetMeeting presentations as an ineffective method of knowledge transfer during the on-site aspect of this investigation. The topic was explored further in the subsequent interviews held two years after the original onsite of the investigation. Both Project Managers were asked how they had found NetMeeting as a medium for providing training on their projects. They both said it had not worked in both instances as the research had highlighted, therefore it was eventually abandoned.

### 6.3.5 Team Intranet Sites

In both embedded case studies, the Irish based team members had their own intranet team pages. Only one team's page contained specific information regarding the Irish-based team members. In that instance, that information was limited to team members' names and e-mail addresses. In the Beta team, the Irish-based team members' intranet site had a Frequently Asked Questions (FAQ) page. A respondent from the same team went on to say: *"I would say that it is not the most effective page [laugh]"*. He went on to clarify that comment:

> "there is some useful information such as XXXXXX commands, how to set up this and how to set up that…every time you learn something new if it is not in there you can stick it in there. So a lot of people can pick it up".

It appeared that effective use was being made of the Irish Beta team page by the provision of relevant information that would have been of specific value to their remote colleagues. The ability for team members to update that information when and as required was of particular benefit. Whether all the Irish-based team members would be inclined to expand the FAQ section was another matter given some team members' reluctance to share information with their remote colleagues.

This was all put in perspective when another respondent from the same team was asked if their team had an intranet page and they replied "*There is no team page on the intranet"*. This highlighted the need, not just for the provision of relevant material on a team site and an effective method to update it. There was also the specific requirement for that information to be broadcast to all team members in both locations.

A respondent described the Alpha team intranet page as: "*Yes it is adequate and there is a lot of information on it"*. Their Far Eastern colleagues also had an intranet page but, as an Irish respondent stated:

> "We have a team page and they have a team page… I looked at it (the [Far Eastern] page) and I have not looked at it again. I do not know what is there."

This attitude was not restricted to the Alpha team. A member of the Beta team stated when asked if their Far Eastern virtual team colleagues had an intranet page: "*There may be I don't know, I have not looked"*. This again highlighted the need for awareness and specific training to support the effective utilisation of tools to facilitate successful communication in the virtual team environment.

A communication tool that was not available was video conferencing. When asked about its use, the respondents' replies are summarised by the following statement: *"If we had videoconferencing I think that might help, if we saw those people"*. The desire for video conferencing came from the respondents themselves. They clearly appreciated the difficulties of operating in an environment without the normal collocated visual contact with their remote colleagues. In these circumstances the provision of videoconferencing equipment warranted consideration.

## 6.4 The Need for a Communication Procedure

The correct use or misuse of communication tools has been identified as having a direct impact on the success or failure of virtual software teams. A common misuse of e-mail is to copy and thereby escalate minor issues to senior management, particularly to highlight the failings of remote colleagues or to pressurise them into giving preference to the sender's requests. While there are occasions when relevant individuals (be they management or staff) should be copied on e-mails, this clearly was not the case with some of the situations outlined by the respondents in this investigation.

It has been shown that, where communication tools have been misused, this practice has directly contributed to conflict, alienation, mistrust and a lack of cooperation, between virtual team members situated at different locations. This issue was something the respondents were familiar with and something they highlighted. While it was not identified as a specific problem with their Far Eastern virtual team colleagues, it had and was being experienced dealing with other Far Eastern, North American and Middle Eastern staff. In discussing this topic with respondents typical comments were outlined as follows:

> "We do see that with other teams, with development in XXXXXX and the [Far Eastern country]. They as routine [sic], they copy half the world..."

> "[The Middle Eastern staff] would always copy. If you asked them what time it was they would copy the reply to your manager."

A respondent, speaking about what they witnessed happening to their Project Manager when dealing with North American based colleagues, stated:

> "[The Project Manager] interfaces with them and they do[sic] come across them escalating to the world and his wife if an e-mail was not replied to within thirty minutes"

An important point to emerge from this aspect of the research was that the last statement referred to contact with North American based staff who were former colleagues and had been collocated with the team members who lost their jobs when their part of project was offshored to Ireland. In these circumstances, e-mail was used in an aggressive fashion towards the Irish staff.

It emerged from the analysis of the data that a documented communication procedure was not in place and one was required. Without clear guidance and direction it was acceptable for people to use, misuse or not use communication tools when and how they saw fit. There were no clear boundaries on what practices and behaviours were considered acceptable or unacceptable. While cultural differences existed between nationalities, they should not have been an excuse for tolerating rude or aggressive behaviour toward remote colleagues in any location. Specifically, with reference to e-mail, it would have been of value to outline in broad terms when it was appropriate and inappropriate to use it as a tool to communicate. It would also be helpful if it outlined when senior management and other individuals not directly involved in issues should be copied on e-mail.

It was not only for the use of e-mail that a documented communication procedure was required. As a respondent stated regarding Instant Messenger and the reason why they were not using it: *"I was just starting up with it and I don't understand the etiquette that goes with it, if you are supposed to respond immediately".* Clear guidelines on when it was appropriate to use the telephone would also have been helpful, given the Irish team members reluctance to use it. An effective, documented and comprehensive communication procedure was required to address all aspects of virtual team communication.

## 6.5 The Need for a Common Vocabulary

Given the communication problems outlined in this chapter, it was not surprising to discover there was a specific need for the adoption of a common vocabulary between sites. The experience level of some of the remote team members was very limited and included a large number of graduates. In these circumstances it should have been anticipated that they would not be familiar with the specific organisational terminology for artefacts, deliverables, procedures, steps, practices and acronyms. When asked if there was a common vocabulary between sites that their remote colleagues understood, the respondents' replies were similar to the following statement: *"No it is all new to them, because I know they asked what functionality freeze was at a call last week"*.

A Project Manager when asked about this issue stated:

> "[A Trainer] would have gone through it as part of the training with them [the Far Eastern team members]. During process training they would have gone through a lot of the terms and a lot of the documentation and stuff and explained all of them to them".

This training was provided over a number of conference calls utilising NetMeeting. The comments received from the respondents regarding the knowledge their remote colleagues had of these terms would support the assumption that this training had not been successful.

The extensive use of acronyms exclusive to the particular industry was also an issue. The use of these acronyms is so common it is difficult for new employees who have not worked in this industry before to initially gain knowledge of them all. The Irish-based team members understood these difficulties, despite having had direct access to a mentor and a large number of experienced colleagues in Ireland to answer their queries.

> "It does take a while to get to know what the acronyms mean. I remember the first time I looked at all the [these] acronyms I felt I would never learn them."

The Far Eastern team members only had a limited number of experienced personnel at their location to provide answers to their questions and even their knowledge was not extensive. If clarification was required from an Irish-based mentor or team member there was only a limited opportunity for such an exchange to take place. Information regarding acronyms was stored in a number of locations, but the respondents did not consider what was available adequate. Furthermore, the researcher was informed that the Far Eastern staff may not have been aware that this information was available.

## 6.6 Technical Ability, Knowledge Transfer and Training

There was a clear difference in the level of technical ability between the Irish-based staff and their Far Eastern colleagues. The Irish operation was well established and had a continuous staff-training programme in place. The average experience level of the Irish team members was four years. Most of the Irish staff had gained their experience within the organisation's testing department. All the Irish team members had benefited from an extensive in-house training programme. The Irish-based teams' competitive advantage lay in a combination of their technical knowledge and practical experience.

In the Computing World Far Eastern Software Centre, the testing operation had been established for two years. Over that period they had carried out straightforward, well-partitioned, offshored software testing. This work had been undertaken successfully and the Computing World Far Eastern Software Centre had been assessed, as a whole, as Capability Maturity Model (CMM) Level Five. They had operated with an initial testing staff of thirty for the first year . In the previous few months that figure had increased and the Far Eastern based testing staff numbered one hundred when the on-site aspect of this research was undertaken. In these circumstances it was to be expected that there would be mixed technical skill levels within the organisation as a result of this rapid expansion. As a respondent stated:

> "A lot of them had very little experience and were just fresh from college or fresh from another job in a different sector or different company".

Staff recruited in the Far East did not have the opportunity to gain the level of technical expertise required for undertaking complex virtual team testing prior to joining this organisation. The existing experienced Far Eastern based staff were also limited in their exposure to complex testing given the nature of the work they had previously undertaken.

Without effective knowledge transfer and training, distributed software development cannot succeed. This training cannot take place by osmosis particularly in a virtual team environment when team members are culturally, linguistically, temporally and geographically distant. An effective strategy was required to be put in place to ensure that this goal was successfully achieved. Computing World, as a whole, was committed to the provision of effective training and knowledge transfer for all their staff.

In Ireland, a combination of in-house training and mentoring was provided. This commitment to training was also maintained for existing staff and provision was made on an on-going basis when the need and opportunity arose to provide relevant training. This took the form of internal courses and sourcing of relevant external training when the technical expertise was not available in-house. Irish based new starts were provided with mentoring. This process was outlined in detail by a Trainer:

> "People are assigned a mentor so they work with the mentor... The mentor is here, someone who is an existing team member in the test department who is experienced in doing PRs [Problem Reports], FRs [Fault Reports], that kind of things...That new person can contact their mentor by phone or e-mail or just come over and ask a question...Every time they will have some kind of interaction."

The combination of formal training and mentoring proved a successful training strategy for the Irish based staff. The Irish based division had responsibility for the provision of training for their remote virtual team members. The method employed to train the Far Eastern team members was to replicate the Irish collocated training procedure as far as possible. A respondent outlined the strategy as follows:

> "For [the Far Eastern country] we are trying to do the same thing... We would have done a lot of training with them ourselves. [A Trainer] would have given them training over a number of days on all the different aspects of the process (using conference calls and NetMeeting). "

A Trainer from another team who also provided conference call and NetMeeting training stated:

> "We held workshops by NetMeeting… there were technical problems [with] the phone system; the phone connection to [the Far Eastern country] is not the best".

As has been articulated conference calls and the effectiveness of the use of NetMeeting to provide remote training was clearly in doubt.

The value of face-to-face training was appreciated. The provision of on-site training in the Far Eastern country was made available when possible.

This specific approach has been recognised as valuable in a distributed environment. A Trainer from Ireland travelled to the Far Eastern country where he had responsibility for providing formal training courses to existing staff and new starts. His assessment was that some of the staff he came in contact with had very limited experience and technical knowledge. Linguistic and cultural issues also came into play. Specifically, their knowledge of English was varied. The ability to understand the language in which training is provided in is a paramount requirement to facilitate successful knowledge transfer. As with the NetMeeting conference call training, he also found it very difficult to assess the effectiveness of the training he provided. As he stated:

> "There was limited feedback received from the training given. Some of the [Far Eastern] team members say nothing in case they say the wrong thing or appear stupid. Again this may be a cultural issue not to express an opinion or due to the fact they just did not understand what had been presented".

Provision was made for the Far Eastern team members to have Irish based mentors. This practice was outlined as follows:

> "Then they [the Far Eastern team members] were identified for feature work depending on what feature work they were given. Then they were told who the person in Ireland would be helping them out".

Mentoring works well in a collocated situation, but it is directly impacted by cultural, linguistic and specifically temporal difference in a virtual team environment. It was not clear what would happen if a Far Eastern team member needed to ask their mentor an urgent question when the mentor was not available. Given the limited scope in the overlap of working hours between locations this meant that direct access to mentors was quite restricted. The only option the Far Eastern based team members had was to e-mail their mentor and wait for a response. The earliest that a response could have been received would have been at the end of the Far Eastern team members' working day.

An additional problem with mentoring was the reluctance on the part of some of the Irish based team members to communicate knowledge to their remote colleagues for fear of losing their jobs to them. As a Project Manager stated:

> "People are hesitant to transfer information or knowledge it is human nature… Yes it is natural everyone is human".

This comment was not expressed as justification for individuals employing such an approach or that the practice was condoned in anyway. It was simply an honest assessment of the impact fear was having and, as a result, some of the Irish staff were unwilling to share their knowledge with their Far Eastern colleagues.

The most successful form of knowledge transfer took place when a number of Far Eastern team members travelled to Ireland for training. This approach was considered very effective by the Irish staff in general and it offered the opportunity for the development of some aspects of a social relationship between normally remote and, in some instances, disaffected colleagues. Not withstanding that, a social outlet was not provided for the development or fostering of such relationships. *"It is very difficult to dislike people that you meet and get to know."* The respondents' views on this subject are represented in the following statement:

> "Engineers came over from [the Far Eastern country] recently and there has been a lot of training on that. It has gone fine; it is better when Engineers come over to Ireland for the week they get much more out of it. That works better."

The training provided to the Far Eastern virtual team members who travelled to Ireland was considered the most effective approach to employ. When the question was asked: how the provision of training could be improved, the following statement summarises the respondents' replies:

> "Seriously I would probably bring more [Far Eastern] team members over here for training and send Ireland people over there."

Naturally there was a limit on the number of Far Eastern staff that could travel for training to Ireland, given the level of expense involved. A key goal of that training strategy should have been to ensure that those who made the trip to Ireland leveraged that experience to the full. To achieve this objective, the training programme should have incorporated the opportunity for the development of social as well as professional relationships between the trainees and their Ireland based colleagues. On returning to the Far Eastern country, those who travelled to Ireland for training should have been utilised to provide on-site training and pass on the information they received to their colleagues. These individuals may also have been suitable for selection as liaison personnel between sites. The benefits of utilising this role was identified by in their GSD research which they also carried out within the Computing World corporation. The liaison role was being assumed informally and mention was made of the contact the people had with these individuals on their return to the Far Eastern country.

> "Do I know people over there?... Well the people I have met personally here yes – [those] who [sic] I have had a lunchtime chat with".

Given the importance of effective knowledge transfer and training to the success of the virtual team strategy it was surprising that the Irish-based management, trainers and staff had very limited or no access to information on the technical ability of their Far Eastern colleagues. A skills database did not exist and the need for one was not recognised by the Irish management. Project Managers did have access to Curricula Vitae (CV) and a brief presentation of their Far Eastern staffs' backgrounds. This, in the Project Manager's view, was inadequate. As a result they had to instigate ad hoc meetings with Far Eastern managers when they visited Ireland to determine individual team member's technical ability. Similarly the staff in the Far East did not have access to information regarding the technical experience or expertise of their Irish colleagues. This lack of information impacted on both locations, as there was no direct mechanism to help identify subject matter experts when technical support was required.

### 6.6.1 How the Problems with Training were Addressed

As discussed in Section 6.3.4.1 during the on-site aspect of this investigation, the provision of training for the Far Eastern-based team members on both teams had been identified as a problem. This issue was discussed in detail with both Project Managers, when they were interviewed two years after the original onsite investigation. When NetMeeting was abandoned another strategy for providing training was required. Similarly, it was recognised (as highlighted by this investigation) that the remote mentoring of the Far Eastern staff by their Irish colleagues had its limitations.

To address these issues, both Project Managers came up with the same solution. This was to bring as many Far Eastern team members to Ireland for training as possible. As this was an Irish-based decision, a large portion of the Irish budget for both projects was spent in implementing this strategy. This was in addition to the Far Eastern team members who came to Ireland for training during the on-site aspect of this investigation.

On their arrival in Ireland, the respective Project Managers insured that the Far Eastern staff received intensive training, which was monitored. The objective was to prepare these individuals to act as liaisons and mentors for their colleagues when they returned to their Far Eastern country. This approach had limited success, but was sufficient to allow both projects to be completed.

## 6.7 Conclusion

In this chapter, communication and its implications for virtual team operation have been considered at length. The importance of having a reasonable opportunity to effectively communicate has been outlined. The impact temporal distance has on communication has been discussed. The importance of the ability to communicate and linguistic competency in the use of English, combined with the need for communication training, also emerged from the analysis of the data. The tools that facilitate virtual team communication have been reviewed and their use evaluated in the light of the results of this study

The key factors to emerge from the analysis of communication were language, tools, knowledge transfer and temporal issues (see Figure 6.1). An important related issue is that, regardless of how extensive the choice of communication tools in a virtual team environment, ultimately what is key is that people need to be motivated to utilise them. Of equal importance for their effective use is that relevant training in how to communicate in a virtual team environment is provided. The provision of adequate information is also essential. The lack of and the requirement for a documented communication procedure, a common vocabulary and the need for effective skills management have been highlighted. The importance of knowledge transfer and its associated problems have also been presented and discussed at length. The analysis of the data also identified that communication directly impacts on motivation, information, training, skills management and project management. It is important to note that fear is a direct obstacle to effective communication and must be acknowledged and addressed as such.

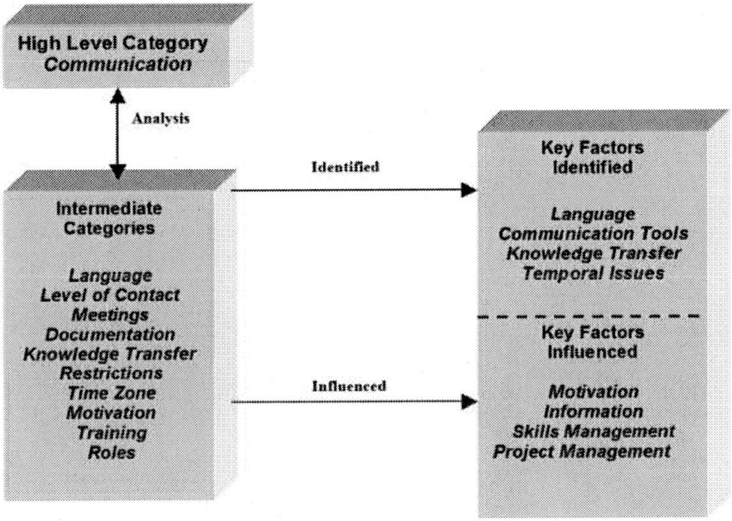


Figure 6.1: The Analysis Of The High Level Category Communication

# CHAPTER SEVEN

# PROJECT MANAGEMENT

## 7. Project Management For Virtual Teams

A key point to emerge is that a collocated project management strategy is not effective in the virtual team setting. To facilitate successful virtual team operations, specific project management related issues need to be addressed. This necessitates a change of emphasis and orientation in the development and implementation of a virtual team centric project management strategy. As a result, this strategy has to be virtual in its focus and broad in its method of operation. To achieve this objective, the first step is the recognition of what specific factors need to be addressed. There is the requirement to determine what they are, why they are relevant and where, how and why they impact.

### 7.1 Project Management in The Organisation Researched

The project management strategy implemented by the test operation for the management of their virtual testing teams proved less than optimal. In previous offshoring endeavours, the division's project management strategy had been considered adequate. This was not the situation with the project management of their virtual team strategy and two key factors were identified:

- Effective Partitioning
- The nature of the work offshored

For successful offshoring/outsourcing, effective partitioning of work should be undertaken. This had been the case for the previous projects offshored by the test operation and had ensured there was a limited requirement for communication and coordination between sites. The second factor was the nature of the initial work which was offshored. Due to its limited complexity, it facilitated effective partitioning. The management of the organisation had described this as '*grunt*' work (meaning it was straightforward and required only basic technical skills to be executed correctly). This resulted in the need for limited external supervision and minimum interaction between staff at both locations. In these circumstances where only straightforward offshoring had been undertaken, a single site project management strategy at both locations had proved adequate. These factors helped to explain the success of the earlier offshored projects.

These findings also provided an explanation for offshoring problems only being encountered when the virtual team strategy was implemented. The exportation of the unmodified collocated process was not suitable for the successful operation of the virtual teams. It was evident that the project management strategy that was put into practice clearly replicated the collocated approach. There is a clear requirement for management to understand and handle the level of complexity involved in offshoring.[1] This has particular relevance when implementing a virtual team strategy. It was evident that this important issue had not been recognised by the management of the testing operation.

As a result of the analysis of the data and the problems which were identified, it was clear the project management strategy implemented had to be reassessed in the light of the needs of the virtual environment. Specifically, it needed to acknowledge and address the key factors, issues and variables that directly impacted on the operation of the virtual teams. Therefore, there was not only the requirement to plan, monitor and control cost, time, quality, pervasive risk and productivity on each project. There was also the necessity to plan, implement and monitor communication and coordination related activities within the teams. Specific policies and procedures to facilitate and monitor communication between sites were required. The provision of training at both locations in methods of effective communication and the use of communication tools also needed to be addressed.

The impact of cultural diversity on the operation of the projects needed to be determined, monitored and steps taken to tackle the relevant issues identified. A coherent team had to be developed from a culturally diverse and geographically dispersed group who were required to work as a single

---

[1] Jonsson, N., D. Novosel, and J. Lillieskold. Successful Management of Complex, Multinational R\&D Projects. in Proceedings of the 34th Annual Hawaii International Conference on System Sciences 2001. Maui, HI: IEEE Computer Society.

unit to achieve specific testing targets and goals. Procedures should have been put in place to facilitate and monitor the level of cooperation between team members in both locations. There was a clear need for the development of trust between remote colleagues.[2] A key issue in this regard was the requirement for measures to be taken to address the palpable fear felt by many of the Irish-based virtual team members that their jobs would be offshored to the Far East. This was a serious problem which needed to be acknowledged and addressed by Senior Management.

There was a requirement for policies and procedures to be drawn up for the establishment and operation of the virtual teams that insured adequate visibility into the relevant activities and outputs of the respective team members at both locations. There was also the necessity for the clear and unambiguous articulation of roles and responsibilities for all team members. A clearly defined common vocabulary for key milestones, procedures and processes should have been produced and implemented which was clearly understood by team members at both locations. To be effective, a successful virtual team project management strategy needs to address, monitor and control all these additional areas, variables and issues.

## 7.2 The Organisational Virtual Team Strategy

GSD and virtual team literature has focused on the operational aspects of distributed development and its associated problems. In this investigation, not enough emphasis had been placed on informing and securing Senior Management support for a sustained virtual team strategy. Prior to embarking on such an approach there is a need for Senior Management to be made aware of the true advantages, risks and disadvantages of undertaking such a strategy. Based on accurate information their support can be successfully achieved and maintained.

The success of any complex organisational strategy is dependent on the level of sustained support provided by Senior Management for its implementation and operation.[3] To achieve effective support, it is required that the success of such a strategy is directly linked to the attainment of

---

[2] Herbsleb, J.D., D.J. Paulish, and M. Bass. Global software development at siemens: experience from nine projects in Proceedings of the 27th international conference on Software engineering. 2005. St. Louis, MO, USA ACM.

[3] Humphrey, W.S., Managing The Software Process Series The SEI series in software engineering. 1989, Reading, Mass. USA: Addison-Wesley.

organisational goals and objectives. With regard to securing the required support for this approach, it is important that the implementation of the strategy will, in fact, facilitate the achievement of these goals and objectives. The reason why and how this will be accomplished needs to be realistically defined and clearly articulated to Senior Management to gain their support. It also needs to be considered that, in a number of situations, GSD has failed[4] or produced disappointing results.[5]

Cost saving is often sited as a key factor for organisations embarking on such a strategy.[6] As stated by a respondent who had access to such information within the organisation researched, the real cost of a Far Eastern Engineer was half that of an Irish Engineer (not the much quoted *two fifths*). Even at half the cost this was not an effective figure on which to base a realistic comparison. The Irish team members had on average four or more years' testing experience within the organisation. As a result, they had technical knowledge and experience of numerous aspects of testing which their Far Eastern colleagues did not possess.

The Irish based Engineers' technical knowledge and relevant experience was reflected in their dependability and productivity levels. This needed to be factored into the equation to provide a realistic comparison. It is important to appreciate that the Irish based staffs' technical and productivity advantage was time limited. The productivity gap between staff at both locations would decrease as the Far Eastern based virtual team members' technical knowledge and experience increased. The implementation of an effective project management strategy could have been utilised to address these issues and speed the closure of the gap.

Wage and infrastructure costs are not the only elements involved in the implementation of a virtual team strategy. There is also the effect that such a strategy can have on the staff at the location where the work is offshored from - and the negative impact this can have on their level of

---

[4] Laplante, P.A., et al., The Who, What, Why, Where and When of IT Outsourcing. IT Professional,, 2004. 6(1): p. 19 - 23.

[5] King, W.R., Developing A Sourcing Strategy for IS: A Behavioral Decision Process and Framework. IEEE Transactions on Engineering Management, 2001. 48(1): p. 15 – 24.

[6] Bass, M. and D. Paulish. Global Software Development Process Research at Siemens. in Proceedings of the International Workshop on Global Software Development, International Conference on Software Engineering (ICSE 2004). 2004. Edinburgh, Scotland.

cooperation and productivity. These factors all need to be considered when calculating the true cost of undertaking such a strategy.

### 7.2.1 Risk

Risk is a key factor which needs to be specifically addressed in the virtual team environment, while pervasive risk should be incorporated into all well planned software projects. One of the reasons articulated for the large number of failures of software projects in the nineteen-nineties was directly attributed to the fact that managers were not taking measures to correctly assess and manage risks.[7] Globally distributed development projects carry additional high risk exposure. These include the risk of delay or failure due to linguistic, cultural difference, motivation and temporal distance. These issues need to be recognised and addressed.

In these circumstances the area of risk management needs to be considered in the light of a globally distributed virtual team environment. *"Risk management deals with potential problems unique to a specific software project".*[8] The political risk of offshoring mission critical activities to remote locations was not considered by management in the division researched.

Furthermore, with specific regard to The Far East, the element of risk involved in the operation of a North American multinational organisation in a predominantly Muslim country needed to be recognised. Equally, the ethnic and religious make up of the Far Eastern country's population and the historical conflict which has taken place between these groups and the implications this may have for future political stability also required due consideration.

An additional relevant area which this research has highlighted was the risk involved in the strategy of having the Far Eastern staff work long hours because they seem to be prepared to do them. This was directly due to their cultural reluctance to say no when asked to do extra work. The consequence of this strategy was the loss of a large number of experienced personnel that the organisation had invested time, effort and money

---

[7] Keil, M., et al., A Framework for Identifying Software Project Risks. Communications of the ACM 1998. 41(11): p. 76 – 83.

[8] Thayer, R.H. and R.E. Fairely, Software Risk Management, in Software Engineering Project Management, R.H. Thayer, Editor. 2000, IEEE Computer Society Los Alamintos, California, USA. p. 195 - 202.

training. The stage of the project when their departure took place dictated the level of negative impact that such a strategy incurred. To resolve this, the Test Manager had forbidden this practice within the testing division.

This problem arose as a direct result of the management of the testing division not being aware of the cultural implications of working with Far Eastern virtual team members. The implementation of the virtual team strategy also introduced risks within the Irish operation. Staff were seriously demotivated and, if the job market in Ireland had been better, people would have left the organisation. In these circumstances, a collocated risk strategy which addressed the elements of a single site software-testing project was not adequate. As a consequence, project management and risk management required additional effort and activities to achieve their objectives in a globally distributed virtual team environment.

To undertake and implement a sustainable virtual team strategy, realistic expectations must be put in place for the projects. The relevant implications need to be clearly articulated and understood by all the relevant parties and projections have to be based on achievable targets. Having secured Senior Management support, there is a need for that support not just to be expressed in a tacit manner. This needs to be coupled with the provision of resources both financial and technical to establish and support a process and project management strategy that can specifically address the needs of the globally distributed virtual team environment.

## 7.3 Infrastructure

To support a virtual team strategy, investment in key infrastructure is essential. This issue needs to be considered at an early stage, during the selection of an offshoring location. The availability of a dependable electrical supply or the hardware to ensure that, when interruptions in supply take place, an alternate power source is available, needs to be addressed. Of equal importance is the availability of an adequate telecommunications infrastructure. This includes dependable Internet connections, infrastructure and bandwidth. This research has highlighted the problems associated with an inadequate remote telecommunication system and its impact on routine communication. This also had a negative impact on training and knowledge transfer.

Once basic infrastructure has been put in place the next step is the sourcing of common tools for the locations involved. This ensures the interoperability of cross-site operations and artefacts. This had taken place with the virtual teams researched. A relevant, related issue which arose in this area was that, while some tools are supported by the manufactures in North America and Europe, they may not be covered when they are located elsewhere. This was highlighted when a piece of equipment sent out to the Far Eastern country from Ireland developed problems. The relevant Project Manager discovered that, because of its location, it was no longer covered under its normal warranty. As a result, the equipment had to be returned to Ireland to have it repaired. It is important that, when tools are selected for use in a virtual team environment, the situation regarding the geographical areas covered by the warranty is clarified. When necessary, additional cover should be secured if available. Where that is not possible, alternative tools should be selected which can provide such cover.

An essential element of virtual team operation is the selection and implementation of an effective configuration management system.

"For global software development there is no tool more important in the software engineering category than SCM [Software Configuration Management]". (Carmel 1999)

Within the test operation this was recognized and an effective documented configuration management system was in place for all the relevant documentation, problem reports and artefacts. The organisation made provision for communication by supplying a large selection of communication tools for the virtual teams. As highlighted by this research, having access to these tools does not guarantee that they will be used, but they are an essential requirement to operate successfully in a virtual environment. With proper motivation, training and management, their effective use can be the lifeblood of a successful virtual team strategy.

## 7.4 The Virtual Team Process

Once adequate infrastructure is in place, the organisation implementing a virtual team strategy needs to adopt a common and effective virtual team process. In some globally distributed environments this approach might not be appropriate - for example, in situations where collaboration is temporary and prompt results are urgently required. With the virtual teams researched there was the specific need for agreement on how the work was to be carried out and the objective should have been the development of an effective shared and agreed process to achieve that goal. Such a process needs to be based on the requirements of the projects, the virtual team environment and the needs of the staff at both locations. "*Organizations must reassess existing processes for use in a distributed work environment*". This includes the need for more formal methods of collaboration and communication, given the loss of informal communication methods.[9]

### 7.4.1 The Need for Effective Conflict Management

The specific requirement for conflict management, particularly in a virtual team setting, has been recognised.[10] When the respondents were asked about a procedure or method for conflict resolution, a typical reply was: *"If you asked the question I would say people would probably say 'I don't know'. There is probably an official procedure there somewhere"*. In the collocated situation, an informal procedure was in place if an individual could not resolve an issue and/or there was serious conflict with another member of staff, they contacted their Project Manager directly. This step was only undertaken in extreme situations. *"If I could not resolve it one to one with the engineer, I would go straight to [the Project Manager]"*.
When conflict management was discussed with a Project Manager, they outlined the resolution mechanism that was in place in their virtual team. *"There is probably a HR [Human Resources] related mechanism, stuff like that - for serious stuff."* When the Project Manager was asked if the HR mechanism was used, they stated: *"They are not really used"*. They went on to outline their experience when dealing with conflict within their team as follows:

> "I have come across different situations with different people and conflicts. To be honest, it is very difficult to say there are rules. I have gone through all the training, I have gone through the conflict management training and the things you should do... Depending on the conflict

---

[9] Herbsleb, J.D. and R.E. Grinter, Architectures, coordination, and distance: Conway's law and beyond. IEEE Software, 1999. 16 (5): p. 63 – 70.
[10] Sabherwal, R., The role of trust in outsourced IS development projects. Communications of the ACM, 1999. 42 (2): p. 80 – 86.
Paul, S., et al. Understanding Conflict in Virtual Teams: An Experimental Investigation using Content Analysis. in Proceedings of the 38th Annual Hawaii International Conference on System Sciences, 2005. HICSS '05. 2005. Hawaii.

> involved and the situation… in some cases I have had situations where the two people literally work it out themselves…"

This strategy may well have been effective in a collocated situation where staff have the opportunity for regular face-to-face contact and, on that basis, can work their problems out. This is not the case with remote colleagues within virtual teams. In this setting, "*there must be some mechanism for handling conflict resolution and someone who decides that resolution*". On a positive note, it was of value that the Project Manager had received specific training in conflict management; but it is clear that this was only for managing conflict in a collocated environment.

It is important to remember that there are different types of conflict. Some are open and easy to recognise. There is also another type of conflict which is not blatant, but is still there, festering. This was particularly relevant to this research, given the attitude of some of the Irish based team members toward their Far Eastern colleagues. This was compounded by the Far Eastern cultural aversion to conflict and their reluctance to express their opinions, or even openly disagree with their Irish colleagues. When unreasonable requests or behaviour were experienced, their approach was to ignore it rather than confront it. This had particular relevance to the effectiveness of the informal procedure which was in place, which another Project Manager went on to outline as:

> "With reference to the remote sites, an informal procedure exists. There is an escalation procedure, which is specific to the project. It depends if it is a personal thing, or 'I cannot continue my project because I am not getting a response from this person'. That would come up as part of the weekly report we get from the team in the Far East. As part of that they would highlight any risks, any issues and stuff like that…There is not a formal mechanism."

The Project Manager had not received training in the culture of their remote team members so it was a case of learning as they went along. Their statement that there was no formal mechanism in place summed up the reality of the situation. This along with the other factors outlined highlighted the requirement for the testing process to be evaluated and modified in light of the needs of both locations.

### 7.4.2 Process Ownership

In the virtual team situation there is a clear need for a well-defined and documented process to be in place. This process requires the specific requirements of the virtual team environment to be taken into consideration. The Alpha team had been in operation for a year and a half. The collocated process had simply been exported to the Far Eastern virtual team members. It had not been modified to address any of the issues which have been highlighted. What was of particular note was the attitude of the relevant Project Manager when asked if their remote staff had any input into the process or if negotiations regarding the process had taken place with them. The answer was: "*We exported the Irish process out to them and there was no negotiation, or need for negotiation.*" This view was echoed by a senior member of the team when responding to a similar question. They went on to say they did not see why their remote colleagues should have any input into the process. This highlighted the fact that, after a year and a half, the Far Eastern team members were still not perceived as partners; rather they were seen as a resource to simply offshore work to. Their views and requirements regarding the exported process were not sought or considered. It was clear that exclusive ownership of the process lay with the Irish team members. This approach did nothing to develop an effective cooperative virtual team environment. Sole ownership of a software development process by team members at a single location in a virtual team setting can lead directly to the alienation of team members at the other site. As a direct result, this can negatively impact on the whole area of virtual team cohesion and the long-term effectiveness of a virtual team strategy.

Good software practice recognises that process ownership and development are best placed with those who are closest to the process.[11] This clearly was not the situation in this case. This is particularly relevant as the Far Eastern virtual team members were part of a CMM Level Five division and the Irish Test operation was CMM Level Three. The premise of a CMM Level Five organisation is that "*the entire organization is focused on continuous process improvement*".[12] Therefore, it is surprising that input was not sought from experienced Far Eastern team members as to how the process could be improved. In this context it is important to state that while the majority of the remote team members were graduates and new starts there were some experienced Far Eastern team who could have been consulted.

---

[11] Fitzgerald, B. and T. O'Kane, A Longitudinal Study of Software Process Improvement. IEEE Software, 1999. 16(3): p. 37-45.

[12] Paulk, M.C., et al., The Capability Maturity Model: Guidelines for Improving the Software Process. SFI Series in Software Engineering. 1997, Reading, MA. USA: Addison-Wesley.

To address the issue of process, there was the need for the establishment of common goals, objectives and rewards across both sites. A key element in implementing this approach is the development of dual ownership of the process. The input of staff at both locations must be sought, encouraged and valued. There was a need for the process to be totally reengineered to incorporate these issues.

The requirement for the definition and implementation of a common vocabulary, which included the clear definition of artefacts and deliverables, had been identified. This was particularly relevant given the problems encountered with training and knowledge transfer. There was also the need for agreement across sites on the achievement of jointly formulated milestones and it would not have unreasonable to have anticipated that such agreement would have been in place.

A key goal of the CMM Level Two Software Project Planning key process area is that "*Affected groups and individuals agree to their commitments related to the software project*".[13] A collaborative element which addressed this issue should have been incorporated into the development of a shared and agreed process, which specifically tackled the needs of the virtual environment in which it operated. In the Alpha team the project milestones were "*written in stone*" as the Project Manager put it. As a result the Far Eastern team members did have the opportunity to highlight if they were unable to meet the milestones, but they were set for them without discussion or negotiation.

## 7.5 Team Structure and Organisation

Another important aspect to the success of a virtual team project management strategy is the implementation of an effective team and organisational structure. Establishing an organisational structure involves the creation of roles, relationships and rules which can facilitate effective coordination and control. In the software industry, the overall objective of the implementation of a collocated and virtual team structure is to facilitate the successful management, coordination, and operation of the teams. In the virtual team environment, it is necessary that this structure is cognisant of and addresses the additional variables that need to be

---

[13] Paulk, M.C., et al., The Capability Maturity Model: Guidelines for Improving the Software Process. SFI Series in Software Engineering. 1997, Reading, MA. USA: Addison-Wesley.

considered. The importance of documenting this structure and providing access to this information is an important step. The purpose of this exercise is to allow all staff to understand their and other people's roles and responsibilities within the project.

The options for the geographical distribution and structure of the virtual teams researched were outlined by a Project Manager as:

> "You have a choice; you can either have a full remote team just managed from here [Ireland] for example. You can have a team that is half and half. You can have a team that is mostly here and a small number of the people remotely located."

They then went on to outline the specific geographical structure of their own virtual team and the problems associated with its operation:

> "There is a larger team in [the Far Eastern country] and the team is getting smaller here… I suppose it is more difficult to get a structure in place that allows you to have two teams working together… As you have to have it right for what the Irish Engineers are responsible for versus the remote Engineers."

The second Project Manager stated about their team: *"But we have a very small Irish team, but a big [Far Eastern] team so the balance is actually very right"*. The balance of having a small number of Irish-based team members and a larger number in the Far East was considered the ideal objective. The Project Manager went on to outline the rationale for implementing such an approach:

> "The strategy is to utilise and leverage the local [Irish] experience and combine that with cheap and more efficient labour costs in [the Far Eastern country], that is what we are trying to do".

The *'very right'* size of the teams researched equated to around eight team members based in Ireland and eighteen to twenty in The Far East. Size is an important element in virtual team operation. Virtual teams are, in general, larger than collocated teams. As a respondent stated regarding their experience of working as part of a virtual team:

> "I think there are things that slow it down and I don't think it is a totally efficient way to work … I think any management who think that OK we need to do twice as much work let's get a similar size team at the other side of the world to do the work. I think they are missing a small bit of the overhead involved in it."

Overall team size can impact directly on the effective operation of a virtual team.[14] Equally the number of virtual team members located at one specific geographical location versus another can negatively impact on team relations. This was highlighted in this research by the fear that was expressed by a number of Irish based team members at the large number of their colleagues who were located in the Far East. The strategy of having the majority of the team located in the Far East was perceived by many of the Irish staff as the precursor to the loss of their jobs to the Far Eastern location.

Additional issues to emerge from this research were the problems associated with having a large number of inexperienced team members located in a remote time zone. This directly resulted in a limited opportunity for synchronous support from their more experienced colleagues. This had particular relevance when those colleagues were tasked with providing essential training, knowledge transfer, mentoring and support. It had a negative impact on the efficiency of the operation of the teams as a whole. It also placed a large strain on the team members at the off-shoring location who were expected to provide support to a large number of inexperienced remote colleagues:

> "[The management] could maybe not go for a big bang effect. Maybe they could start off with a small team over there. It is easier to build up knowledge with a couple of people and then allow that team to grow over a certain amount of time and that does not leave such a huge training burden on the home team. Which is what we are having to spend a lot of our time doing at the moment."

### 7.5.1 Dual Reporting

Given the management structure that was in place for both the Alpha and Beta teams, an area of possible concern was, while the Far Eastern Managers reported to the Test Manager and the relevant Project Manager, they also reported directly to Far Eastern Senior Management. The possible negative implications of dual reporting had to be considered. This situation is not unusual when operating in a cross divisional or multi-organisational virtual team environment. Where these approaches are implemented there is always the possibility of one of the party's involved

---

[14] Bradner, E., G. Mark, and T.D. Hertel. Effects of Team Size on Participation, Awareness, and Technology Choice in Geographically Distributed Teams. in Proceedings of the 36th Annual Hawaii International Conference on System Sciences. 2003. Hawaii.

giving undue priority to their divisional or organisational needs, rather than the requirements of the virtual team and the project they are working on. Specifically this can have serious implications if a Manager at one location coordinates the virtual team members they have responsibility for in a particular manner that is of benefit to their own division or organisation and not in the best interests of the virtual team as a whole.

When the matter was discussed with the Project Managers, they acknowledged the importance of this issue. They made sure that they had regular contact with their remote managers to ensure they were undertaking the activities that were required. This approach has been recognised as good practice for the operation of distributed software project teams. In a virtual team environment there is a need for continuous visibility into all aspects of the team's operation.

A positive procedure which was in place was highlighted by a Project Manager who received a questionnaire to complete on a regular basis to rate the performance of their Far Eastern team Manager. This was a good practice, as the Far Eastern Manager was aware that their work was being rated. It was also an incentive for them to focus on the effective operation of the Far Eastern team to cooperate with their Irish-based colleagues. This research has highlighted that team level problems in regard to support and cooperation were more likely to emanate from the Irish-based team members than those in the Far East.

### 7.5.2 Achieving Common Goals, Objectives And Rewards

An important factor for successful software virtual team management is that common goals and objectives are put in place which are agreed and understood by all the team members, regardless of location. The team members are required to focus on the achievement of these goals and success has to be measured by their accomplishment.[15] To actively foster this approach, a key objective should be that the team is seen as an entity in its own right regardless of the location of its team members and its performance should be judged accordingly. On this basis, success should be evaluated on the operation of the team as a single unit and rewards should be based on that success and equally shared between locations.

---

[15] Casey, V. and I. Richardson. Virtual Software Teams: Overcoming the Obstacles. in 3rd World Congress for Software Quality. 2005. Munich, Germany.

What may be considered a reward in one culture can be seen as inappropriate to those from another. The idea that '*money talks*' in every culture is far too simplistic an approach. Cultures place different values on different types of rewards. In many Western cultures, money is seen as the primary reward mechanism. In contrast in some Far Eastern cultures, status and group achievement can be considered more of a reward than money. In general, in the Far Eastern country where the remote virtual team members were based, people do not value the pursuit of wealth for its own sake. It is important for management to understand the cultural motivation of the different team members and to identify and apply appropriate rewards in each situation when and where relevant.

As well as cultural diversity, the economic situation and the income tax laws at each site need to be taken into consideration when determining the specific level and form of reward provided.

## 7.6 The Organisation and Distribution of Work

Virtual teams, by their very nature, are collaborative and highly dependent on effective cooperation and communication to operate successfully. They are directly impacted by distance. Therefore, they are vulnerable to the negative factors and problems associated with globally distributed software development. As a result, the organisation and distribution of work across virtual software teams is a critical task that management must address. The objective should be to distribute the work so that the advantages of GSD are leveraged and its negative factors are minimised. This can be achieved by implementing one or more of the three types of approaches to task allocation illustrated in Figure 7.3. They are module based, phased based and integrated, 'follow the sun' task allocation strategies.

Modularisation which entails effective partitioning is a key concept in the effective organisation in globally distributed development and virtual team operation. Modularisation is a concept based on the work of Parnas (1972), who defined it as: *"In this context 'module' is considered be a responsibility rather than a subprogram"*.[16] This statement highlights that a modularised design decision can be effectively utilised for the division of labour. It is this division that creates the need for and places limits on

[16] Parnas, D., On the Criteria To Be Used in Decomposing Systems into Modules. Communications of the ACM, 1972. 15 (12): p. 1053 - 1058.

the requirement for interdependence between individuals and teams in the development of software products. In the GSD and virtual team environment, this is achieved by the effective partitioning of work into modules which have a limited requirement for interaction between geographical locations and have a well defined functional whole.

This approach can translate directly into independent or semi-independent units that may be developed at different geographical locations, with the minimum of interaction between teams and/or team members. This has particular relevance for offshoring where the partitioned parts of the work can be undertaken entirely at the remote location. Once the requirements are clearly defined and understood, the infrastructure and training are provided and effective co-ordination and reporting structures are in place, the work, in many ways, can be undertaken in the same manner as a collocated project. Prior to the implementation of the virtual team strategy, this well-partitioned, modularised approach had successfully been utilised by the Irish division for offshoring some simple basic testing operations to remote locations.

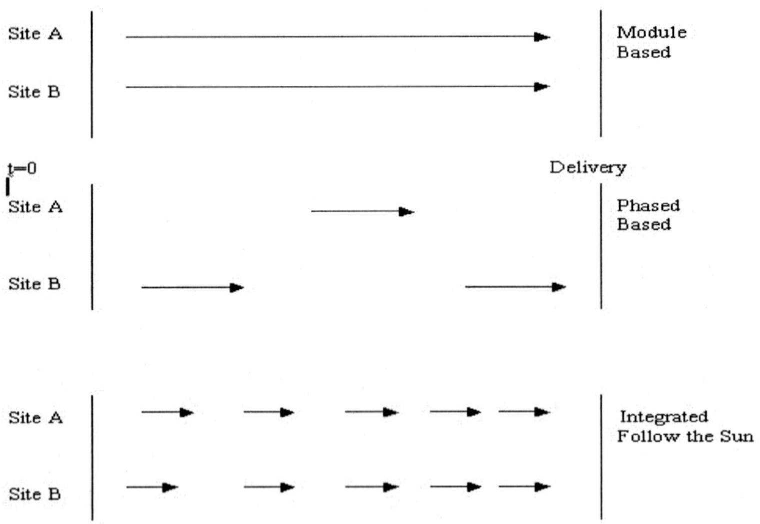


Figure 7.1: Types Of Task Allocation

With reference to a phased-based approach, different, discreet phases in the development cycle can be undertaken at different locations. This can be successfully implemented where each phase is relatively independent and those who carry out the work clearly understand what is required at each stage. As a result, each phase can be successfully completed with a minimum need for communication and cooperation between locations.

The integrated, or follow-the-sun approach, is a strategy that allows temporal difference to be leveraged.[17] Unfinished work is passed between locations to utilise tools and time differences fully. The objective is to achieve 24 hour development, where possible. Where this can be successfully undertaken, it allows the benefit of shorter development and testing cycle times[18] and, as a result, it can provide the opportunity to be first to market. The successful implementation of a follow the sun approach is dependent on the process and the ability of engineers to document and communicate the following to their remote colleagues:

- What work has been completed?
- All the relevant information on how that has been done.
- What additional work needs to be carried out by those at the next location?

Given temporal difference, this often has to take place utilising asynchronous tools, due to the limited or nonexistent overlap in working hours between locations. As a direct result of the impact distance has on distributed software development, there is a negative impact on communication, cooperation and coordination. The actual results from an integrated strategy are often small and fall short of what was anticipated.

The transition stage of each of these task allocation strategies is the weakest link in this approach. For its successful implementation, a clear understanding of requirements is essential and work needs to have been carried out in a documented fashion. This information must be communicated to the next tester to undertake the work successfully. In Computing World (Ireland) Ltd., as part of the testing process, these types of task allocation approaches were incorporated into the alternative virtual team testing strategies which were considered:

---

[17] Espinosa, A. and E. Carmel. Modeling Coordination Costs Due to Time Separation in Global Software Teams. in ICSE Workshop on Global Software Development. 2003. Portland,Oregon, USA.

[18] Raffo, D., S.-O. Setamanit, and W. Wakeland. Towards a Software Process Simulation Model of Globally Distributed Software Development Projects. in Proceedings of the International Workshop on Software Process Simulation and Modeling (ProSim'03),. 2003. Portland, Oregon, USA.

- Subsystem or system (Modularised).
- Feature or non-feature (Phased).
- Execution or preparation (Integrated).
- Senior Tester in one site hands on to another in the other location (Integrated).

Within the virtual teams researched, the partitioning of tasks was also dependent on the location of the testing hardware. In the Beta team, a respondent stated:

> "All the requirement- based testing is going to The Far East and all the system-level testing is going to be done in Ireland. So when I say system-level testing, I mean anything that needs to be done re hardware, because we have the [equipment] here."

The position was that some aspects of the testing had to be undertaken solely by Irish-based team members due to the location of some of the test equipment. Other testing activities were shared with their Far Eastern colleagues.

The long-term objective for both teams researched was to implement a follow-the-sun strategy. That said, there were doubts expressed by some members from both teams as to the possible success of this approach and the following statement is representative of those views:

> "I have heard this utilisation [follow-the-sun], but I don't really see it happening. I can't see any huge advantage."

The testing strategy implemented for the Alpha team was well partitioned and was mostly feature based. As the Project Manager of the Alpha team stated: *"I allocate some features completely over to them [the Far Eastern team members]. If it is a big feature then it can be half and half"*. The testing strategy did contain some large features which were shared across sites. The follow-the-sun strategy which was being implemented was also feature-based as a respondent outlined as follows:

> "You might have one feature in Ireland and one feature in the Far East and even though sometimes there is… a huge feature that there are several people working on. Generally you would have maybe one person per feature. It is not the case that you would be handing over work and you would be worried that you would be duplicating work."

As the relevant Project Manager stated, as a result of this approach, *"they do not need to interact as much"*. This was a good practice in the circumstances, given the communication, cultural and the other issues which negatively impacted on the operation of the virtual teams researched.

As outlined earlier in this chapter, an additional factor which both teams' Project Managers and Team Leaders had to contend with was their limited knowledge of the Far Eastern staff's technical ability. This was a key factor which had to be considered when allocating tasks. Another very important aspect of this issue was that there was no formal assessment method in place that could be utilised to determine the success of remote staff training. As outlined, all the indications were negative relating to the effectiveness of the training provided by conference calls and NetMeeting. There was "*a work it out as you go along*" approach to evaluating the technical ability of remote staff which impacted on the efficiency of any task allocation strategy that was implemented.

## 7.7 Team Cooperation And Teamness

Cooperation between virtual team members is essential for effective virtual team operation. The term '*teamness*' [13] has been broadly defined as the ability of individuals to collectively collaborate and work effectively as a team.[19] Carmel has identified the loss of teamness as one of the five centrifugal forces which result from virtual team operation. Distance has a negative impact on the level of teamness between remote colleagues, coupled with the fact that it is difficult to integrate geographically remote and culturally diverse groups into a single team. It is not difficult to appreciate why, in these circumstances, problems can and do arise.

In this environment, to facilitate collaboration and cooperation, there is a need for trust to be developed between team members.[20] Trust is established through building relationships between team members. When this is successfully achieved, the results can be a motivated and cohesive team with a common purpose and shared goals and objectives. While this is the intention, the reality is that a globally distributed virtual team environment directly militates against the establishment and operation of

---

[19] Glaser, A., S. Fu, and M. Tumelty, On Site: Growing A Participatory Programming Environment Communications of the ACM 2004. 47( 6): p. 27-29.

[20] Royce, W., Software Project Management : A Unified Framework Object Technology Series, ed. Booch, Jacobson, and Rumbaugh. 1998, Reading, Mass. USA: The Addison-Wesley.

effective virtual teams. Fear has been identified as a key inhibitor for the establishment and operation of cohesive and motivated virtual teams. The specific fear that the whole operation will be offshored from the outsourcing location to the remote site needs to be acknowledged and, when and where possible, addressed. This important topic will be considered in more detail in Chapter eight.

### 7.7.1 The Impact of Offshoring On Working Relationships

The impact offshoring had on the working relationships between those at an outsourcing location and those offshored to, emerged from the analysis of the data. A Project Manager outlined their own and their team's experience of dealing with the former colleagues of team members who were dismissed in North America and whose project was offshored to Ireland. This situation was more extreme than that identified between the Irish-based staff and their Far Eastern colleagues, but it contained the same constituent elements. The negative impact offshoring had on trust and cooperation clearly emerged.

Initially, one of the projects researched commenced with North American and Far Eastern based virtual team members. The North American based team members were very experienced, but six months into the project they were dismissed and their part of the project offshored to Ireland. The Project Manager outlined their experience of the hand over and subsequent dealings they had with their North American based colleagues regarding the project. The Project Manager stated: "*I have had a brutal experience...*"

> "We did not have the basics. We did not even know what the [product] looked like. So it was horrendous I do not know how we survived it... we actually did a very good job..."
>
> "Another thing was that I would have liked a lot more support... management support [at the North American offshoring location]. I found it was more negative then positive. I found I was fighting things, rather than trying to make it easier for me. I had the opposite. In fact, I don't think anything was made easy."
>
> "Going through it, I was more compassionate towards the [North Americans] and what they were going through. I got real aggressive calls from people and stuff. It was really, really horrendous."

The respondent was asked if those people should have been brought to book for the treatment they gave to the Project Manager and the Irish team. The question was also asked if the Project Manager had complained about this to the management at the offshoring location. Their reply was as follows:

> "Well I did [complain], I had one issue with my peer, supposedly my peer and XXXX got hired by the XXXX division and is still around. That was just the worst experience I ever had. It was the most unnerving thing I ever had. Basically we just started from scratch. We could rely on nobody. The previous team structure was such that we could not reuse anything they had… I just thank God that I had the calibre of engineer I had."

> "We could not find test plans; we could not find basic stuff; we could not find test reports. XXXX would not give me a test report that was issued the previous week. That is how bad it was. XXXX was just a psycho: 'Oh! I have lost it'. So we started from scratch"

As outlined, there were numerous problems which the Project Manager and the Irish-based team had to contend with. They were required to undertake a project which was offshored after it had commenced and the previous team were dismissed. The previous team had not developed nor implemented a defined process. The Irish-based Project Manager and team were required to work directly with and were expected to rely on former colleagues of the staff that had been dismissed. There was a lack of knowledge and information about the product and there was an absence or '*loss*' of relevant documentation and artefacts from the last team. There was a clear lack of support from the remaining staff at the offshoring location. There was no cooperation or trust between the North American based staff and their Irish-based colleagues.

What the Irish-based team did receive from that quarter was aggression, hostility and uncooperative behaviour. In fact, as outlined, rather than cooperation, obstacles were placed in their way. The most serious aspect of this was the lack of support from management at the offshoring location. Complaints were made about the behaviour of individuals and they were ignored. The Project Manager described their dealings with the management at the offshoring location as fighting against the Irish-based staff rather than supporting them and nothing was made easy. This was an on-going problem and, for over a year, the Project Manager tried to shield their Irish team members from its worst excesses.

These statements were made by a very capable manager with wide experience and an impressive track record of achievement within the organisation. As stated they initially endeavoured to shield their Irish-based team members from the problem.

> "Personally there was only so much I could solve on the team's behalf ... also I was protecting the team an awful lot in the first year from things... Then when I opened that up to them, once they were a year into it, they then began to see how brutal this project is..."

This provided an explanation for the negative comments made by Irish-based team members regarding dealing with their North American colleagues. As one member of this team stated:

> "Maybe [North Americans] may need some training in culture as in how we work? I think they are the ones that come across sometimes as being very aggressive".

Another Irish-based team member made excuses for their North American colleagues' bad behaviour, as they recognised it was as a direct result of the number of jobs they lost and the way their colleagues had been treated.

The important element here, one which is consistent with this research and with a separate independent study undertaken in this area by the researcher, is the fact that the fear of/the result of outsourcing/offshoring can lead to a mistrust and resentment, which manifests itself in uncooperative and, on occasion, aggressive behaviour toward those at the remote location. A serious aspect of this situation was the management at the offshoring location had done nothing to address these problems and it appeared as if such behaviour was condoned and considered acceptable.

To achieve a collaborative virtual team, the first step is to realise the extent of the potential problems and factors that have to be addressed. A cohesive virtual team does not just emerge - its establishment and operation requires careful consideration, planning and management. Direct steps need to be taken to address the specific problems which the virtual environment impose. While the Project Manager and Team Leaders need to assume responsibility and take measures to ensure that this very important area is adequately covered, the support of senior management is required if this is to be successfully achieved.

In the organisation researched, a major step taken to address these issues was the provision of an ex-gratia payment to the Irish-based staff for the

implementation of the virtual team strategy. This did not provide an effective incentive and proved counter productive, as it added to the fears of the Irish-based team members that their jobs would be exported. Morale was further undermined by the use of the cost and productivity mantras. The Project Managers were not in a position to convincingly reassure their teams of their future job security even though they and the Test Manager did their best to do so. Their efforts were specifically undermined by visiting Senior Management's public change of emphasis from a clear unequivocal commitment to the future of the Irish operation to one that was dependant on costs and productivity.
Given the professionalism of the Irish Project Managers, they would not tolerate their Irish-based staff openly treating their Far Eastern colleagues in such a flagrantly aggressive and confrontational manner as the Irish team and Project Manager were treated by their North American colleagues. That stated, the fears, mistrust and the desire not to communicate or pass on relevant knowledge was evident among some of the Irish team members, but it was expressed in a more latent manner. These fears needed to be overcome and, as outlined, this was best addressed by developing relationships and trust which were clearly lacking between team members in both locations and in both teams researched.

### 7.7.2 The Lack of a Single Team Approach

A single virtual team vision was not in place and, in a number of situations, even the Project Managers referred to their Far Eastern virtual team members as the other team. This was reinforced by the fact that joint group meetings of Far Eastern and Irish based virtual team members did not take place. The need for such meetings was recognised by some of the team members themselves and their views can be represented by the following statement:

> "At the moment we have group meetings, but it is a group meeting for Ireland and a group meeting for [the team members in the Far East]. I think we need to move closer to us all knowing what everyone is doing."

When asked if anything was done to develop a single team relationship between the sites - to integrate the Far Eastern - and Irish-based team members into a single virtual team - a respondent stated: *"Am... not that I know of"*. Another respondent stated: *"I think if we foster more of the one team attitude, I think that is very important"*. It was clear that a one team approach was not being effectively developed and it was required. The need for a one team approach was appreciated by a Project Manager, who stated:

> "I am trying to create an atmosphere where we are actually working as one team and some of the stuff we have done, I think, has helped. Like have some of the engineers over here and they work with the engineers here so they know who is who."

In isolation, this was a totally inadequate approach which was highlighted by the Irish-based virtual team members themselves given it lacked any social team building aspects.

## 7.8 Project Visibility

Due to its geographical and temporal impact, distance imposes a direct barrier to virtual team project visibility. The implications of this barrier must be recognised and measures taken to overcome it, to facilitate effective virtual team operation, coordination and management. Project visibility is required to and from all locations where virtual team members are situated. As a Project Manager stated, regarding managing a virtual team: "*Visibility is key*". There are two essential areas which project visibility directly tackles. It is an important element which facilitates a shared understanding of a project's purpose, process and what the desired outcomes and artefacts are. It facilitates effective project coordination and control. It also allows for the provision of information on what has been achieved and what still has to be done.

The first area visibility needs to address is that team members at both locations have access to relevant information and support, which allows them to understand clearly what their roles and responsibilities are.[21] They need to be able to determine what these roles involve and what and how they are required to carry them out. As outlined earlier, there is a need for a common unambiguous vocabulary in all team locations. This is required to cover activities, the process, documentation, milestones, deliverables and artefacts. Information on team members' experience, technical ability and a procedure and mechanism to identify subject matter experts should be in place. Due to temporal difference, this information and support needs to be formally documented in a manner that can be easily accessed by team members in different geographical locations. Calendars and

[21] Whitaker, K., Motivating and Keeping Software Developers. Computer, 1997. 30(1): p. 126 - 128.

clocks showing all public holidays and the time in the other sites where team members are located should be prominently displayed or be easily accessed. The team intranet page should contain photographs of all team members and should outline some brief information about them. This should include their name and the correct form of address as in their first name or friendly name. There is no room for ambiguity in this area if successful relationships across sites are to be established.

The second and more traditional project management role visibility plays is the overview it provides into the operation of the team and the tracking of the project. The objective is to have sufficient visibility to monitor team effort and performance and to determine project status. As a result, when and if required, effective and timely preventive action may be undertaken to address potential problems. Given the geographical and temporal distance between locations, there is the need for extensive visibility into the operation and activities of distributed projects and remote staff.

As a Project Manager stated with regard to visibility:

> " Each of the Senior Testers … it is part of their responsibility to review on a regular basis the progress of the test plans for the features they are responsible for so".

This statement was clarified when, later in the interview, they stated:

> "To be honest right now I think we will sort it out, as we kind of have [sic], as they start executing to a schedule. I would have been finding it very hard to gauge over the last few months, because they are in a learning mode. It is very hard to gauge how they are getting on. I know I would not have had that comfort factor to say yes they are OK."

This particular project was at an early stage and the Project Manager appreciated the need for visibility. While effective tools were being utilised, their limitations were recognised. The Project Manager went on to state: *"It would be good to have someone out there to monitor progress"*. What was of concern was the Far Eastern team's lack of a track record and the limited information that was available regarding their technical competency. The Project Manager went on to state: *"For the projects that are kicking off now we will be midway through some of the newer projects by the time we really get feedback on how well they can deliver"*. A Team Leader responsible for monitoring the progress of the Far Eastern team members concurred with this view when they said:

*"Time will tell if I need more visibility if the thing falls over."* With effective visibility, which is key in a geographically distributed virtual team environment, there should be no need to wait until *"the thing falls over"* for corrective action to be taken.

When visibility was discussed with another virtual team's Project Manager they stated: *"I don't want it as I have too much to do already"*. While the coordination and day-to-day project management activities should not rely solely on a Project Manager it is an area that they ultimately have responsibility for and they need to ensure it is adequately addressed. The next question the researcher asked was: did their Team Leaders have enough visibility and the reply was as follows: *"Yes they do, my Team Leaders do have enough visibility."*

It was of interest to note that a senior member of this team stated the following, regarding the activities of their remote colleagues:

> "We hear very little from [the Far Eastern team]."
>
> "We have had very little visibility into what they are doing. We are trying to improve that."
>
> "Ya, it's hard to get the information where they are at and where they are going and when they think to finish, that kind of information. It is hard to get information from these people. Now I have the feeling that they are not feeding this information back to us."

A clear responsibility for effective project management is to ensure that there is ample visibility into all relevant aspects of the project. This was clearly not the case in this situation. Whatever the Project Manager thought, at team level, effective visibility was clearly lacking.

Ongoing visibility into the operation of the project team and project status is not only relevant from the coordination perspective. It also has wider implications for the team as a whole. Information on progress needs to be transmitted to all team members at regular intervals, regardless of location. This makes available relevant information on what has been achieved and what has still to be completed. This provides an important overview of the current status of the project. It also provides pertinent information regarding interdependency issues to all relevant parties. It can help foster a cooperative approach and a sense of shared responsibility between team members.[22] It is necessary that this information is formalised and regularly effectively disseminated. This is particularly important due to the loss of the opportunity for formal and informal face-to-face interaction between all team members.

## 7.9 Conclusion

In this chapter the role of the project manager has been defined specifically in the virtual software team context. In the organisational setting, the initial success of basic offshoring was contrasted with the difficulties which arose with the implementation of the virtual team strategy.

The key factors to emerge from the analysis of the intermediate categories and project management were: risk, true cost, tools, technical support, partitioning, reporting, process, defined roles and responsibilities, skills management, technical support, team selection, information, cooperation and visibility (see Figure 7.2). In addition all the intermediate categories and key factors identified have relevance to effective virtual team project management. The negative impact that fear can have on effective project management is considerable. This is particularly relevant with regard to developing trust and cooperation between remote team members.

An important point which has been highlighted by this investigation is that the responsibility for successful software project management is not the sole domain of one or more individual Project Managers. It is the responsibility of the management team as a whole, which includes Senior Management, Team Leaders as well as the Project Managers. It requires a concerted effort from all those involved to address and indeed leverage the issues that directly impact on the operation of virtual teams, to manage successfully and deliver effectively a virtual team-based project.

---

[22] Powell, N.G. and B. Posner, Excitement And Commitment: Keys To Project Success, in Software Engineering Project Management, R.H. Thayer, Editor. 2000, IEEE Computer Society Los Alamintos, California, USA. p. 380 - 387.

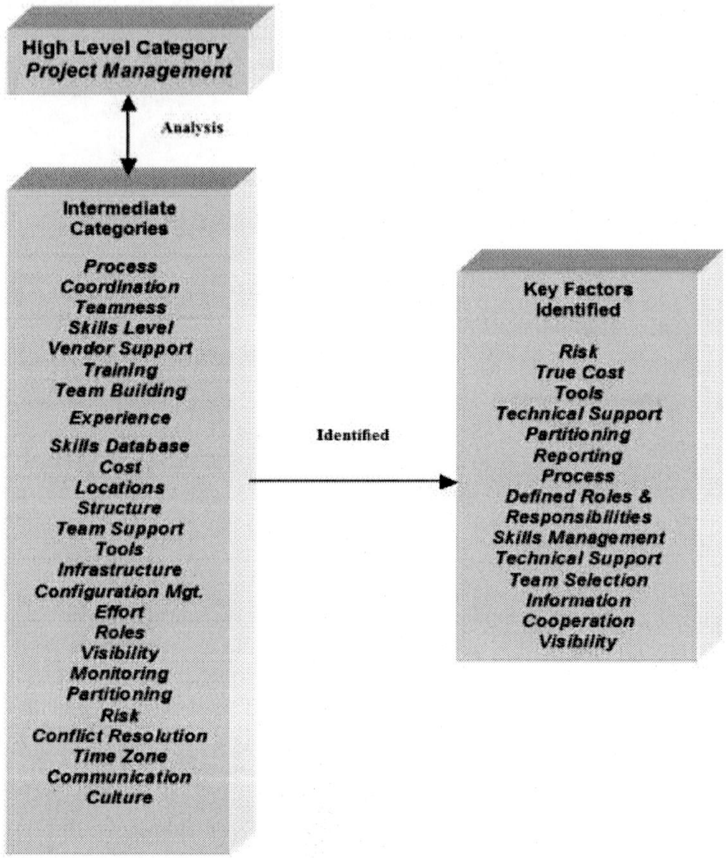


Figure 7.3: The Analysis Of The High Level Category Project Management

# CHAPTER EIGHT

# FEAR

## 8. The Impact of Fear on Virtual Team Operation

The initial research and onsite participant observations identified the existence of a definite level of unease and apprehension among the Irish based virtual team members. It soon became clear that this arose directly from the implementation of the virtual team strategy. The Irish staff genuinely feared that their jobs would be offshored to the Far East. This was confirmed by direct observation and discussions with both management and staff. A large number of Irish based team members on both teams articulated their own fear of this happening or knowledge of the existence of this fear among their colleagues. As a result of further analysis it became clear that this was a key factor which had serious implications for the operation of the virtual teams as a whole.

### 8.1 Background

To appreciate the full implications of fear and its properties and dimensions in the context of this investigation it is important to understand the background of the situation researched. Ireland has a formally regulated labour market. As a result Irish employees have after a period of one year of permanent employment a legal right to recourse if dismissed without due cause. This is outlined in detail in the Unfair Dismissals Act.[1] In addition, when an employer wishes to reduce their staff numbers there are strict rules which apply under the Redundancy Payments Act.[2] The legal situation is that, when positions are offshored from Ireland, the staff can be forced to accept a severance package. Therefore, while Irish staff were protected from being summarily dismissed, they were not protected from their jobs being offshored.

---

[1] Oireachtas, The Unfair Dismissals Act 1977 (Amended 1993). 1977/93.

[2] Oireachtas, Redundancy Payments Act, 1979 1979.

### 8.1.1 The Parent Organisation's Approach to Offshoring

The Irish based management and staff were familiar with the offshoring strategy of their parent organisation. As outlined in Chapter seven the members of the Alpha team were working on a project which had been offshored to Ireland. Originally, a North American based team undertook the work. The transfer to Ireland took place in the middle of the project and the experienced North American based team were dismissed. As a result there was no formal project handover between sites. In fact, there was resentment expressed toward the Irish team members from the former colleagues of the team that had been dismissed. The relevant Project Manager used the word *"horrendous"* five times to describe the experience of dealing with their North American based colleagues as a result of undertaking the offshored project.

It was relevant to note the reaction of one of the Irish respondents who was a member of the Alpha team when discussing what it was like to deal with their North American based colleagues' uncooperative and at times, aggressive attitude: *"But I just think maybe they have lost a lot of jobs. I would not blame them really; you know a lot of their friends have been let go. I can understand why they would feel so badly treated."* A clear point to emerge from this statement was this person's acceptance of what, in normal circumstances, would be considered totally unacceptable behaviour. This was solely based on an appreciation of how those individuals in North America felt and therefore reacted as a result of their colleagues' jobs being offshored.

Given the lack of cooperation and outright aggression that the Irish based team were subjected to from their North American colleagues, this was an interesting response. This reaction had to be taken in the context that the Irish based team members now feared the offshoring of their own positions. As a result this helped them to understand some of the reasons for the uncooperative behaviour and aggression they had been subjected to.

The respondents' long-term view of their future with the organisation is summarised as follows:

> "The way the world is going we will not have any jobs left here. I think with a virtual group that is what is at the back of most people's minds, is that now there are 18 people over in [the Far East] and 8 over here. The

> scales are tipping their way more than it is ours. So it is always at the back of our heads."

### 8.1.2 The Experience Level of the Irish Based Staff

When discussing the advantage provided by the technical ability and experience of the Irish based testing staff a respondent stated: *"There are good experience levels and some good people here".* They then went on to say:

> "The experience level we have here only lasts for so long. It is good for a year or so until a team somewhere else builds up their experience... I get the impression... at a management level the calibre of the people here is not such a huge factor. A resource is a resource and they are probably right nothing we do is rocket science everything we do can be picked up."

The respondent went on to highlight the age and experience profile of the Irish based testing staff as an area of concern:

> "I just look at the way it was when I started here eight years ago. XXXX [location in North America] felt like what this feels like now. There was a lot of thirty something's, forty something's working … they did have an awful lot of experience. You know you would be a little bit in awe. They would all be in senior positions and they all seemed to have strategic input rather then technical input. I guess that is where we are now, since then they have let a lot of people go in XXXX (location in North America). It is nearly a hindrance you are nearly top heavy when you have that. In a sense that is where I see it going... it is not that easy to pull out of here, but I sometimes wonder if it is going that way."

Rather than perceiving experience and technical knowledge as an advantage within the corporate organisation, it has, on occasions been a precursor to dismissal. The strategy of downsizing one location and off-shoring to another is not unique to the organisation researched and is common practice within the software industry.[3]

## 8.2 Implementation of the Virtual Team strategy

When implementing their virtual team strategy the test operation had a recruitment embargo in place in Ireland. As a result all recruitment of new test engineers was only to take place in the Far East. A Project Manager

[3] Cusick, J., How The Work Of Software Professionals Changes Everything. IEEE Software, 2003. 20(3): p. 92 - 97.

stated regarding the embargo: "*I could do with more Irish Engineers, but that is not on the cards.*" Another Project Manager expressed their views on this issue as: "*My biggest concern at the moment is because there is such a dependency on [the Far East]*". They went on to say: "*We don't hire in Ireland so we have no other choice, but to outsource it*"

The implementation of the virtual team strategy and the Irish based recruitment embargo were both major causes of concern for the Irish staff. Their fears were compounded further by visits from senior management. A respondent summed it up as follows:

> "They have always said Ireland is a centre of excellence. 'The work you are doing here is brilliant'. The last two people that have been over have not said that. They said who knows? I can't tell you, if it is going to be cheaper to do things elsewhere then that is something we are always going to have to look at."

The message was clear. Up to the implementation of the virtual team strategy the future of the Irish based test operation was secure. After its implementation its future was unclear.

The Test Manager and his Project Managers did their best to reassure the Irish based staff. A Project Manager summed up the situation as follows:

> "I know the [Test Manager] is very strong at conveying his strategy…so all of his managers can put that into place with their teams and convey it to their teams as well. I am not too sure as an organisation we do a very good job of doing that and I think it is outside of test … sometimes you need it at the higher level to address these types of concerns."

Another Project Manager outlined their Irish based team members concerns as follows:

> "They are smart people they can see what is happening. I have communicated very clearly to them their role and [the team members in the Far East] role and how they differ. Some of them do have that concern... To be honest with you, they are very clear I have told them [the Far Eastern] guys are two fifth the price they are and they need to up their value add and they need to deliver and deliver well."

The cost issue was being reinforced as a motivating factor which proved in this case as in others to be counter productive. The cost and productivity mantras "*Engineers are two fifths the cost in the Far East as they are in Ireland*" and " *you must be more value adding to justify you higher salary"* were heard repeatedly. Rather than having the desired motivating effect it only added to the level of fear and concern within the teams. Cost was something the Irish based staff could do very little about. When the on site aspect of the research was undertaken Ireland was the second most expensive country in the European Union for consumer goods and services.[4]

As a respondent stated: "*the Euro now is killing us*". They went on to say that the only reason that their own organisation were still testing in Ireland was because they had the testing equipment centralised there:

> "The equipment is all centralised here, but if the equipment was moved over there, then they could take on the end-to-end. Then we would lose out that is the one thing we have that we can hold on to."

In a similar vein, speaking about another team, a Project Manager stated:

> "I think there is a kind of concern and I know I have spoken to a number of people who have come to talk to me and there is a team dissolved recently here. Well not dissolved they were transitioned into a different team at the moment and the work was moved to a remote team. I think there is a concern that they are going to lose their jobs. They (the jobs) are going to move to low cost centres."

The transition of an Irish based team and the offshoring of their roles was a serious indication of what could have been in store for the rest of the Irish based virtual team members. As a Project Manager pointed out when discussing fear of job loss within their team:

> "[The Far Eastern] team that is now being created within XXX [a technology]. They are all now being trained up. The previous team still exists and they would be very nervous. I think it is that team that would be very nervous. That is the local Irish team… Yes XXXX here is a very big team and the same job can be done in the Far East very cheaply"

The fears and concerns of the Irish based staff were expressed equally across both teams. A sample summary of these fears and concerns are presented here:

> "There are a lot of people who are paranoid that a lot of work is going to The Far East."

---

[4] NCC, NCC Statement of Prices and Costs 2004. 2004, National Competitive Council of Ireland: Dublin. p. 1 - 5.

"I would be concerned that the whole test group would move out to The Far East."

"Nobody knows what the future holds for us, that is what everyone is saying to me, that it does not sound great…Realistically if they (The Far Eastern team members ) do get up to speed then what future have we got … It is all coming down to cost..."

"As more work is being pushed out to [the Far East] we are losing control of what is going on and I get… We are losing control of what is going on and we hear very little from [the Far Eastern team]."

"I know people have said that they reckon there is another two years, or three years in the place."

These findings were discussed and accepted by the Test Manager, but there was an element of disappointment that, regardless of everything he and his Project Managers had done, that this was the situation.

## 8.3 Implications of Fear

The implications of the fear people had of losing their jobs were serious and this was of particular concern and relevance in the virtual team environment. The analysis of the data clearly indicated that fear impacted negatively on the key areas of communication, motivation, cooperation, trust, team building, and knowledge transfer. It had the potential to lead to geographically based conflict between the Irish and their Far Eastern colleagues. It also became clear that this has serious implications for the effective operation of the virtual teams as it impacted directly on the other high level categories identified.

A Project Manager outlined their experience of establishing their virtual team as follows:

"The problem with it is there is reluctance within the team. In fairness everyone is working away with the person over, some people more so than others. I think there is a kind of concern and I know I have spoken to a number of people who have come to talk to me."

That concern was that the testing operation would be totally outsourced to the Far East. These findings were found equally within both embedded case studies.

The commonality of findings between both embedded units of analysis within this case study was a total unexpected outcome. This fact was clearly evident with regard to fear. It would not have been unreasonable to anticipate a marked difference in attitudes to this issue between the Irish based staff who were part of a team for over eighteen months and those who were part of a team which had been in operation for six. In fact what emerged was there was no discernable difference between them. The same level of apprehension and fear were evident in both teams. There was a clear and similar reluctance within both teams to engage and communicate directly with their Far Eastern colleagues. This situation had been highlighted and confirmed by a number of senior members of both teams. It became clear that the length of time the virtual teams were established did not dissipate the level of fear or alienation felt by the respective virtual team members.

### 8.3.1 Fear and its Impact on Communication

A large number of the Irish based staff were reluctant to use the telephone to contact their Far Eastern colleagues on business related issues. When asked to rank the most effective tools to communicate with their remote colleagues the telephone was ranked third by the majority of team members interviewed. This attitude was summed up in the following statement:

> "I think a lot of people are nervous about talking to people in … I would say, have you been in touch with XXXX over in [the Far East]? They would say no… I haven't. I'd think they were more nervous of them more then anything else."

A number of reasons were cited for the Irish based team members' reluctance to use the telephone. They included not being able to determine the first name and surname of their remote colleagues, their ethnic origin and their gender.

> "Regarding dealing with The Far East we don't even know how to determine ethnic origin by their names. We don't even know which name is their first name."

A Project Manager stated:

> "We did not know if they were male or female. The names meant nothing to us and they would probably have been the same with ours… People are hesitant to ring someone when they do not know if they are male or female so they are not even communicating with them."

Similar statements were repeated numerous times regarding the order of the names of their Far Eastern colleagues and this was stated as the reason why the telephone was not used to contact them. The researcher was unable to determine the Far Eastern naming conventions from anyone within the organisation. Therefore he carried out research to clarify the situation and the results turned out to be straightforward. The reason why gender or knowledge of ethnic origin should prevent an Irish team member from speaking to a remote colleague on the telephone was not explained, even though this question was asked on numerous occasions.

The virtual team members located in Ireland and the Far East did not receive any form of communication or cultural training regarding their remote colleagues. They were equally unaware of the naming conventions employed at the others location. The Far Eastern team members experienced similar confusion when they telephoned their Irish colleagues.

> "I have had people addressing me on the phone by my surname and I am not comfortable with it. Clearly they thought it was my first name."

There was also confusion regarding the use of friendly names. The Chinese as a courtesy when dealing with people who speak English often adopt an English name. A respondent summed it up as follows:

> "Then there is the name thing…a lot of them have friendly names. The Chinese adopt friendly names. So you see a mail with a Chinese name on the top and it will be signed at the bottom 'Dave'…and you don't know if you should call them Dave back or use their formal name."

Given that the Irish based team members had dealt with Chinese colleagues on previous projects, it was surprising that this issue led to confusion, or was referred to as a problem. This indicated two possibilities. The first was that this issue had not been previously encountered (which was unlikely). The second was it had previously been clarified, but its relevance had not been recognised and therefore its solution had not been documented.

Other issues raised as to why the telephone was not used to contact team members in the Far East included their knowledge of English, their accent and the quality of the telephone lines. While all these were relevant points, the most common reasons cited for not telephoning their Far Eastern virtual team colleagues was not knowing the correct form of their name and gender.

As a direct result of the reluctance of the Irish based team members to use the telephone there was a reliance on e-mail to raise and respond to day to day issues. This added to the time it took to have work related matters addressed. As a Team Leader stated:

> "It is a frustration for me… I say what is the story with that and they will say that I sent an e-mail yesterday. They need to pick up the phone and that is a problem people don't pick up the phone as much as they should."

The gravity of staff not communicating by telephone was not understood or appreciated by management. As a result nothing had been done to address this problem. The researcher proposed an action research based strategy to clarify and tackle this situation which was opposed by the Irish based virtual team members and management (see Chapter four).

The lesson to emerge from this exercise was that the majority of the Irish based team members in both teams did not want to communicate directly with their Far Eastern colleagues. The only explanation for this and the level of opposition to any suggestion made to improve the situation was that this arose directly from the fear they had of losing their jobs and the desire they had to minimise direct contact with their remote colleagues as a result. It is very easy to resent and dislike someone you do not know personally, particularly if they are a serious threat to your future.

## 8.4 Motivation

Motivation is defined in the organisational setting as "*The mainspring of behaviour; it explains why individuals choose to expend a degree of effort toward achieving particular goals*". It is a key constituent of any successful operation as it is the driving force in the achievement of goals and objectives. This is particularly relevant in the team situation where individuals are motivated to be part of and to make a direct contribution to the joint effort of the team as a whole. The success achieved by a group is dependant on the level of motivation of its constituent members. An individual will value membership of a group based on the level of satisfaction that it achieves:

- Friendship, where the individual like's and is liked by their fellow team members.
- The task, where the person approves of the purpose of the group.
- Status, where an individual wishes to be associated with a group because of its standing within the organisation and the status that association brings.

These are relevant issues given the geographical, temporal, cultural and linguistic distance between virtual team members and the impact these factors have. This was coupled with the fear of jobs being lost to the Far East. If these issues are not addressed they result in real barriers to developing professional working relationships between individuals at remote locations.

To be an effective team member an individual needs to be motivated to make a positive contribution. There was a clear reluctance on the part of the Irish based team members to communicate directly with their remote colleagues. It was noted in the case of the virtual team that had been in operation for over a year and a half that there was very little evidence that personal relationships had developed between the Irish based team members and their Far Eastern colleagues.

While friendships existed between collocated virtual team members this helped to reinforce the '*them and us'* culture. When the team members were asked the question in the questionnaire: *"Do you feel you are all part of the one team, or is there a feeling here that you are one group and the remote team are part of another group?".* The response was generally negative and the perception was there were two separate teams one in Ireland and the other in the Far East. Similar questions were also asked during the interviews which included: Whether the Irish based team members had a personal relationship with their remote colleagues? Whether they worked as a single team or were there in fact two teams? They were also asked if there was a '*them and us*' relationship between locations. This response summarises those received: "*There is a very clear' them and us' situation here in Ireland."*

It was noted the Project Managers did not perceive their virtual teams as a single entity - rather they described them in terms of an Irish team and a Far Eastern team. This was not a premeditated view. Rather it reflected the reality of the virtual team structure and the fact very little was done at an organisational level to foster a single team approach. The Project Managers had their own concerns for the future of the Irish based role in the testing function.

> "I chose and not without thinking about it to...To make sure that we have some element of the core knowledge here as opposed to [the Far Eastern] team knowing all the different areas".

The objective was to ensure that competency in core knowledge essential to the testing process was maintained in Ireland and that it was not totally exported to the Far East.

Ironically, a key motivator for a group is having a common enemy. Unfortunately, it was a very negative form of motivation. By not communicating directly with their remote colleagues as individuals a personal relationship was not developed. In these circumstances it was very easy to perceive their Far Eastern colleagues as a threat. The reality was the Far Eastern based team members had the potential to facilitate the off-shoring of the test operation to the Far East. The Irish team members' realised this and as a result were not motivated to impart knowledge or work closely with their remote colleagues.

A Project Manager summarised the situation in the following way:

> "The problem with it is there is reluctance within the team… So some people are a bit slow to share some of the knowledge they have … People are hesitant to transferor knowledge it is human nature".

A virtual team member was even more candid when they stated after outlining their fears for the future of their jobs *"So there is a kind of a bit of an apprehension toward these people."* When asked if they thought this level of apprehension would be reflected in the fact that people would not help their remote colleagues they stated: *"I am going to keep something back."* This was a very serious statement to make, as this person did not intend to share their full knowledge with their remote colleagues even though they were expected to mentor them. The implication was clear this person was motivated not to share all their knowledge as they considered their remote colleagues a threat to their future employment. As has been stated by a Project Manager, this reluctance to share knowledge was not unique to this individual.

When asked what advantages were offered by the implementation of a virtual team strategy the respondents in general found it difficult to identify any other than cost:

The Irish based team members were not directly motivated to share knowledge or participate fully in their respective virtual teams. As one person described it when asked about sharing knowledge: *"we are forced to do that".* There was no evidence of friendships between locations. The Irish team members believed the overall objective of the virtual team strategy was to export their jobs to the Far East. There was no status related to being part of a virtual team, indeed it could well be the very mechanism for losing their position with the organisation and the status they had already achieved. While it is not essential to satisfy all three characteristics within a group for the membership to be satisfactory and productive. In the case of the Irish-based team members researched none of Handy's elements were satisfied. While the Irish based virtual team members were professionals they were in fear of losing their jobs and this clearly impacted on their level of motivation. As a result they were de-motivated and despondent.

### 8.4.1 "Motivation" In Context

Comparing the results from the data analysis with the work of Maslow (1943) and Aldefer (1972), the key area highlighted was the impact that fear of the offshoring of their jobs to The Far East had on the Irish based team members. It was clear from the Irish perspective that the virtual team strategy negatively impacted all of the sets of needs highlighted by both Maslow and Alderfer.

Comparing the staff and management style of the test operation in Computing World (Ireland) Ltd to Theory X and Theory Y it was clear that the Irish based virtual team members conformed to the Theory Y classification. They were in normal circumstances focused, committed, self-motivated and capable individuals who welcomed responsibility and had a proven track record of successful project completion. They had pride in doing their work and doing it well.

Initially the management style implemented within the test operation appeared to be based on a Theory Y approach to motivate staff to achieve their best potential. This was particularly the preferred approach of the Test Manager and Project Managers and the style they naturally adopted. There was evidence that this had been the situation, but things had changed. What the researcher observed during the onsite aspect of this investigation was a mix of both Theory X and Y. This change in emphasis in management style could be ascribed directly to the problems associated with implementing the virtual team strategy and as a result the Theory X approach was came more to the fore.

While the Irish team members were professionals and genuinely wanted to do a good job, the fear of losing their positions constrained them. This was highlighted by the contradictions in what people said and did. They did not want to share information, or communicate directly with remote colleagues. On the other hand when their Far Eastern colleagues came to Ireland for training they wanted to get to know them and even invited them to join in social activities. This was a real dilemma given that the Irish-based staff were generally friendly, outgoing and - under normal circumstances - keen to share knowledge. The inclination to be sociable was tempered with the fear that the more they shared the more likely it was that they would be out of a job. In these circumstances the predicament they found themselves in can be appreciated.

As a result management were required to implement a Theory X approach to motivate staff. This approach had a negative impact on the day-to-day operation of the Irish based team members who were essentially best described as Theory Y type individuals. The Project Managers understood the position their Irish team members found themselves in and shared some of their concerns. They endeavoured to be as sympathetic as they could be in the circumstances, but they had no choice, but to implement the virtual team strategy.

The preliminary outcome from this research regarding the motivation and the morale of the Irish based staff was discussed in general terms with the Test Manager. He expressed genuine disappointment at the low level of morale within the department, but the findings were not disputed. It was clear that fear had considerable impact on the operations of the teams

## 8.5 Trust

Trust in the organisational setting is defined as the "*reciprocal faith in others intentions and behaviour ... In short we give what we get: trust begets trust, distrust begets distrust*". The importance of trust has become increasingly recognised as a critical element in the successful operation of organisations and specifically of business, professional and employment relationships.[5] Trust is the foundation of successful cooperation amongst

---

[5] Lewicki, R.J. and B.B. Bunker, Developing and mantaining Trust in Work Relationships, in Trust In Organizations: Frontiers of Theory and Research. 1996, Sage Publications: London UK. p. 114-139.
Creed, W.E.D. and R.E. Miles, Trust in Organisations: A Conceptual Framework Linking Organisational Form, Managerial Philsosophies and the Opportunit Cost of Controls, in Trust In Organizations: Frontiers of Theory and Research, R.M. Kramer and T.R. Tyler, Editors. 1996 Sage Publications: London UK. p. 16 - 38.

individuals within and between organisations. It is essential for the functioning of an organisation and the units operating within it. High levels of trust within an organisation improves performance, efficiency, productivity, creativity and the overall results achieved.[6]

With regard to globally distributed software development and virtual teams, trust is a key requirement for success. This point is summed up in the following statements *"Webs of technology and trust link virtual teams"*. *"Yet trust is pivotal in a global virtual team to reduce the high level of uncertainty endemic to the global and technologically based environment"*.[7] These points are further defined by *"Virtuality requires trust to make it work: Technology on its own is not enough"*. This issue of trust clearly emerged from the data during the analysis. As a result this was an area that the researcher had to be sensitive to given the level of impact it had on the operation of the virtual teams.

In a non-threatening situation team trust takes time to build between team members, add distance and it takes longer. The analysis of the data highlighted the lack of trust the Irish based virtual team members felt towards their remote colleagues. Fear was a large constituent in promoting the level of mistrust felt by the Irish based team members, these findings were not unique to this research. When an individual perceives their remote colleague as someone who may be compliant in offshoring their job it is not surprising to see why they are reluctant to trust them. This was not helped by the fact that very little information was coming back from the Far Eastern team members regarding the progress of the work that was sent to them.

A Team Leader outlined the problem as follows: "*I know one of the complaints people have is they have heard very little back from people*." Another team member stated: *"We hear very little from the [Far East]."* A measure of the level of fear and mistrust experienced by the Irish staff was articulated by a respondent as follows.

> "I would say they [colleagues in the Far East] are playing politics with people…I would say how they manage their team over there, there is a lot going on we are not being made aware of…Would they actively be trying

[6] Keyzerman, Y. Trust in Virtual Teams. in IEEE International Professional Communication Conference, 2003 2003. Orlando, Florida, USA.
[7] Jarvenpaa, S.L. and D.E. Lindner, Communication and Trust in Global Virtual Teams. Organization Science, 1999. 10: p. 791 - 815.

to undermine us? I would not say they would be actively saying they were doing it".

Distance impacts communication and therefore negatively impacts upon trust.[8] The lack of trust is also a barrier to communication between sites. An Irish based team member summed up their experience of working on one of the virtual teams and how easy it was to mistrust and blame remote colleagues as follows: *" It is very easy to blame someone you don't see"*

The organisation brought over a number of the Far Eastern team members from both remote teams to Ireland for training. While the focus was knowledge transfer it also offered an opportunity for relationship and trust building to take place. Management saw it purely as a knowledge transfer exercise. Even with the level of fear and mistrust that existed some of the Irish based team members saw this as a wasted opportunity. A team member stated:

> "I think maybe more one to one contact [is what is needed], we have had a couple of the [Far Eastern team members] over here. That helps an awful lot… Sometimes it needs to be thought through more then just putting the body in the room and saying 'ya they will get to know people'. Definitely it makes things easier it makes it more… you are more inclined to do things for people if you know them."

Another respondent outlined the organisation's method of training remote staff when they visited Ireland as follows:

> "They are brought in, nobody tells you they are coming. You are told this guy is working with you for the next month and you are not doing anything particularly interesting."

The respondent went on to state:

> The focus of the whole month was technical and never once was there any talk about… We thought a couple of times about taking them out for a few drinks this kind of stuff, but there was no management ever thought it [sic] …There was absolutely no consideration for team building put into it. It was all technical experience."

The individuals concerned saw the value of developing relationships with their remote colleagues even in the circumstances in which they found

[8] McDonagh, E.F.I., K.B. Kahn, and A. Griffin, Managing Communication in Global Product Development Teams. IEEE Transactions on Engineering Management, 1999. 46(4): p. 375 - 386.

themselves. They invited them out on a number of occasions and if management had organised a social event one respondent stated he was prepared to pay to take part. Clearly management did not appreciate or understand the importance of team building exercises and the development of trust between remote team members.

An additional issue which impacted on the level of trust between sites was that there was very little information available regarding the technical ability of team members in both locations. The Irish-based staff were aware that their remote colleagues were predominantly new hires, but there were some who were experienced engineers. There was no skills database that could be accessed to identify a subject matter expert at either location. Therefore there was no mechanism that would allow the skill level of colleagues to be determined. This was particularly important as Irish based Senior Testers were working with remote Senior Testers and Testers in the preparation and execution of test plans. An Irish based Senior Tester who was in that position stated when asked if they were aware of their remote colleagues' skills level:

> "No not a whole lot now, that is something you are left to work out... You need to work out if the fellow asks you stupid questions. Then you start to think the person is not the most experienced. If the questions are not good that is the only guide."

Another respondent on the subject said:

> "Sometimes what would be helpful is to know if someone was junior or senior you do not want to seem patronising to someone, or give too little information to others and they are afraid to ask you questions as they think they should know what you are talking about.

A Project Manager stated *"I have heard from the development people that some people out there who have been working with us for two years have limited technical knowledge"*. Very few questions were being asked by the Far Eastern based Engineers and there was very limited feedback on the level of progress they were making. As a Team Leader put it:

> "The Senior Testers say start writing the test plan now [said to their Far Eastern colleagues]. 'If you have any questions let me know' and there were no questions, which is a bit scary as this is a very technical area".

Therefore it was difficult for the Irish based staff to have confidence and trust in their remote colleagues technical skills.

## 8.6 Fear and the Power of Knowledge

Knowledge is power and one of the few mechanisms that employees can utilise to defend themselves if they feel there position is threatened, is to withhold knowledge and information. This can take a number of different forms: It can be:

- Reluctance to share knowledge.
- Not responding to request for information promptly
- Only utilising asynchronous communication tools
- Provision of only the minimum amount of information and knowledge
- Refusing to share knowledge
- Not allowing a personal relationship to develop with remote colleagues

These practices had particular relevance for the Alpha and Beta teams as each one was employed in some form or another by some Irish based team members. While the Project Managers on both teams endeavoured to ensure this did not happen, they could not prevent it from happening. As one respondent stated *"I am not going to tell them [Far Eastern team members] everything and let them take my job"*

## 8.7 Were the Irish Team Members Fears Justified?

Given the level of intensity and negative impact fear had on the operation of both the Alpha and Beta teams the question had to be asked: *Were the Irish team members fears justified?* During the onsite aspect of this investigation as discussed in Section 3.2 the rationale outlined to staff for the implementation of the virtual team strategy was that experienced and technically competent test engineers located in Ireland could be partnered with less expensive test engineers in the Far East, thereby reducing costs while maintaining testing rigour and continuing to ensure product quality. Mention was also made of the opportunity provided for 24/7 testing. Clearly the staff were not convinced of the long term viability of both aspects of this approach.

### 8.7.1 Closure of the Computing World (Ireland) Ltd

Two years after the onsite research took place Computing World (Ireland) Ltd. announced that due to the negative performance of the organisation internationally, their Irish operation would closed. The testing function was totally transferred to the team members located in the Far East and the closure of the Irish based operation took place within three months of the announcement.

### 8.7.2 In Answer to the Question

In the light of the events which subsequently took place the fears of the Irish based members of the Alpha and Beta teams were justified. As a Project Manager stated when discussing the closure:

> "At least now we know. We have all being worrying about it and waiting for it to happen for the last three or more years. Now we have a date when we will be out of work. In a strange way it is finally sort of a relief to have a finishing date."

The closure followed the pattern predicted by the staff. The large testing tools were moved to the location of the Far Eastern team members. The number of Irish based team members remained static while the Far Eastern team numbers grew. This was coupled with the Irish team members increasingly having only a strategic and technical input into the testing process.

In these circumstances it was not unreasonable to consider the possibility the virtual software testing team strategy may simply have been a mechanism to facilitate knowledge transfer between Ireland and the Far East. When a Project Manager was asked this question in an interview which took place shortly before the closure of the Irish operation, she replied:

> "I think to stay competitive they (Computing World ) had to get most of the resources to do the work in cheaper countries because their competitors were doing it. So absolutely it was a knowledge transfer."

When asked if she was surprised at the outcome? She answered:

> "not really we could all see where it was going. We hoped we were wrong, but there you are. "

## 8.8 Conclusion

In this chapter the impact fear had on the operation of the virtual teams has been outlined. As a result of the implementation of the virtual team strategy the Irish based staff feared for the security of their jobs. An embargo was placed on recruiting staff in Ireland and the Irish based staff received an ex-gratia payment to compensate for the implementation of the strategy. They were familiar with the organisation's method of operation in other locations regarding off-shoring projects and the downsizing which resulted. These factors added to the level of fear experienced by the Irish based staff that their jobs would be off-shored to the Far East. As this research highlighted this level of fear was not dissipated by the length of time the teams had been in operation. This had serious implications for the operation of the virtual teams as a whole and directly impacted on the other high level categories which this research has identified Fear directly impacted on the level of communication that took place between sites (see Figure 8.1). It specifically had repercussions for the choice of communication tools which were and were not utilised. Regardless of the number of types of communication tools provided if virtual team members are not motivated to use them they will not be used. Corporate Senior Management visiting Ireland compounded the problems experienced due to their ambiguous statements regarding the future of the Irish operation. The outcome was a de-motivated Irish based staff who did not trust their remote colleagues. This was reflected in their reluctance and lack of motivation to share knowledge. This had serious implications for effective knowledge transfer and mentoring.

Fear emerged from this investigation as a central factor. Its influence was wide ranging and it had serious repercussions for the operation of the teams as a whole. It directly impacted on the level and quality of communication that took place between Ireland and the Far East. It de-motivated team members and negatively impacted on their choice and use of communication tools. It was a direct hindrance to knowledge transfer. It had a negative effect on key aspects of project management including team building trust, motivation, coordination, communication, information sharing and cooperation. Lack of knowledge of the culture of remote colleagues and their consequent behaviour added to the level of fear and mistrust which was experienced.

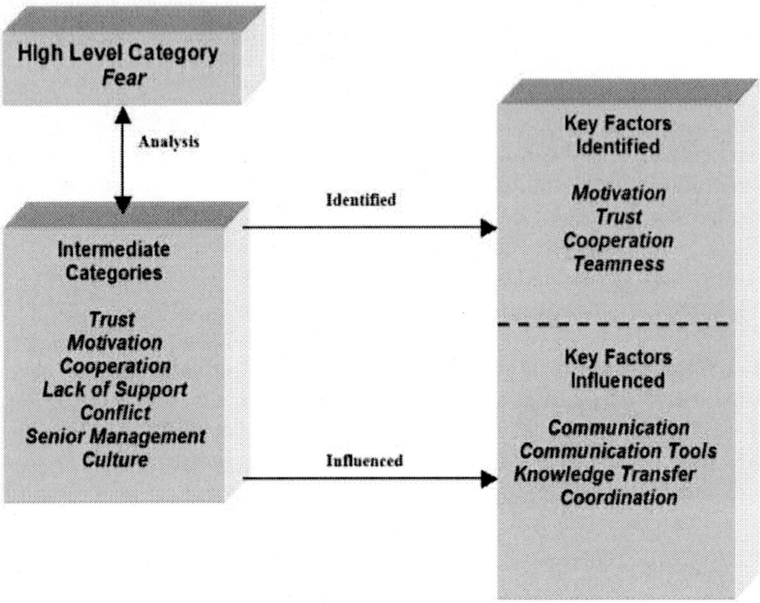


Figure 8.1: The Analysis Of Fear

# CHAPTER NINE

# CONCLUSION

## 9. Findings

As outlined earlier in this monograph the qualitative paradigm was selected as the most appropriate to implement for this study. A case study approach provided the methodology which gave the investigation structure. This was augmented by the use of action research to address the interventionist activities of the researcher. A grounded theory based strategy was implemented for data gathering and analysis. A key aspect of utilising this combination of approaches was to give clear voice to the respondents and thereby provide insight into the operation of virtual software testing teams.

## 9.1 Key Factors Identified

Twenty-five key factors were identified which facilitated and / or directly impacted on the operation of the globally distributed virtual software testing teams researched.

Figure 9.4: List of 25 Key Factors for Effective Virtual Software Team Testing

| | |
|---|---|
| **Communication** | **Skills Management** |
| **Language** | **Team Selection** |
| **Communication Tools** | **Fear** |
| **Knowledge Transfer** | **Motivation** |
| **Culture** | **Trust** |
| **Temporal Issues** | **Cooperation** |
| **Risk** | **Teamness** |
| **True Cost** | **Effective Partitioning** |
| **Tools** | **Coordination** |
| **Technical Support** | **Reporting** |
| **Process** | **Visibility** |

| Defined Roles and Responsibilities | Information |
|---|---|
| Project Management | |

Each of the twenty-five key factors had clearly emerged from the analysis of the data and they were determined as significant in their own right. Each factor should be considered and addressed for the optimal implementation of an effective virtual software team testing strategy. These factors are presented in Figure 9.4.

### 9.1.1 The Key Factors In Context

Virtual software team testing is a complex and difficult endeavour. The key factors identified by this research have a direct impact in facilitating or obstructing the operation of virtual software teams. They are not isolated or simply discrete issues and variables, they impact on and with each other. Some factors are high level and have a direct bearing on many or all of the other factors identified. Others constitute part of or are directly related to some of the other factors outlined. Each warrants due deliberation and consideration in its own right.

## 9.2 Implementation of a Case Study Methodology

An unanticipated outcome from the implementation of the Yin (1994) based case study was when the results from both sub units of analysis (the Alpha and Beta teams) were compared. The differences that emerged between them were very minor. This was an unexpected outcome, particularly given that the Alpha team had been in operation for a year and a half longer then the Beta team.

The same problems with fear, motivation, knowledge transfer, trust, cooperation and culture etc. were common to both teams. Extensive comparisons were made and in the majority of situations the results which emerged from both teams replicated each other. It soon became clear there was very little to differentiate between them.

The main differences this investigation finally identified between the Alpha and Beta teams studied were as follows:

- Length of time the teams were established.
- Technology tested.
- Location of Team Leaders.

- Reporting structure of the respective Project Managers.
- Partitioning of work.

In addition, during the onsite aspect of this investigation a difference in the utilisation of communication tools was identified. The Irish based Alpha team members made extensive use of Instant Messenger when contacting their remote colleagues. They remained as hesitant as their Irish based Beta team colleagues to use the telephone and depended on e-mail as their primary method of communication.

It was of interest to note, that on completion of the Beta team project, the Project Manager stated that her team had continued to be reluctant to use the telephone, but they had in the latter stages of the project made extensive use of Instant Messenger which mirrored the behaviour of their Alpha team colleagues.

## 9.3 Research Questions Answered

The research problem for this investigation has been defined as:
*The identification of the key factors, infrastructure, methods, process and procedures which facilitate and hinder effective globally distributed software virtual team testing.*

The research problem was utilised to frame the original research question:
*How can software testing in a globally distributed virtual team environment be effectively carried out?*
This question was then used as the basis to formulate nine additional relevant research questions. These research questions were addressed by the results from the collection and analysis of the data.

### 9.3.1. Questions and Answers

*How is globally distributed virtual team software testing carried out within the organisation researched?*
The approach implemented for coordinating the virtual software testing teams was the same as that used for managing collocated team. This was highlighted by the following:

- Communication or confliction resolution procedures were not in place.
- Training on how to communicate in a GSD or virtual team environment was not provided.
- Training on the culture of remote colleagues was not provided.

- Mentoring, a key element of Computing World's training procedures was provided by Irish based team members who had an average of thirty-minutes per day official overlap in working hours between locations.
- The process and documentation had not been reviewed in the context of operating in a virtual team environment.
- Team members were not informed when national or public holidays were taking place in their remote colleagues location.

*What areas of virtual team testing have been successfully undertaken and how and why have they been successful?*
The areas of virtual team testing which have been successfully undertaken were as follows:

- The provision of ample testing, configuration management and communication tools.
- A well-documented process was in place, while it had not been considered in terms of the needs of the virtual team environment, it was easily accessed from both locations.
- The lack of monetary restrictions on the Irish side with regard to communicating directly with their Far Eastern colleagues.
- The experience level of the Irish based Section Managers and team members.
- The decision after the onsite research had taken place to bring as many Far Eastern staff as possible to Ireland for training as liaisons and mentors, which directly facilitated the completion of both projects.

These areas were successful as they addressed some of the specific requirements essential to facilitate effective virtual team software testing.

*What problems (if any) do the virtual teams experience and how are they addressed?*
The problems which the virtual teams experienced were numerous they included the following:

- Temporal and cultural distance.
- Fear on the Irish side of losing their jobs to the Far East.
- Trust and motivational issues.
- Refusal to share information with remote colleagues.
- Lack of cooperation and team building.
- Lack of effective methods for training and knowledge transfer.

- Mixed levels of knowledge of English at the remote location.
- Communication Tools not used.

The situation was that these problems were not addressed during the onsite aspect of this investigation. In addition the negative impact fear had on the operation of the teams was considerable.

*What problems (if any) have not been addressed and why?*
In many instances GSD and virtual team based problems were not identified or understood by the management. Where problems were acknowledged, their root cause were not investigated or their full implications appreciated. The problems which were not addressed were as follows:

- Cultural differences and their potential negative impact were not understood.
- The mixed level of linguistic competency with regard to the use of English of the remote team members was not addressed.
- Communication problems while being recognized were not investigated or addressed.
- Motivation and trust were serious problems which were not understood or addressed.
- Mistrust and misunderstandings were common.
- There was a lack of 'teamness'.

In situations where problems were recognised, the Project Managers did their best to address them, but in certain situations they were hampered in their efforts due to the lack of support from corporate senior management.

*How and why do these problems impact on the operation of the teams?*
The reasons for the problems identified were numerous and diverse and had serious implications for the effective operation of the respective virtual teams. An important fact to emerge from this investigation was that the basic problems associated with GSD and virtual team operation were not appreciated or understood by the management of the test department. In addition as a Senior Engineer stated with regard to the introduction of the virtual software testing team strategy:

> "[Computing World's] strategy is to jump into something feet first and worry about how it should be done later".

As a result of implementing a collocated team strategy within in a virtual team environment, the impact of the problems experienced were considerable.

- The telephone was not used to contact Far Eastern colleagues.
- Some Irish based Team Members were reluctant to share their knowledge with their remote colleagues.
- There was a negative impact on motivation, trust, cooperation and coordination.
- There was very limited synchronous communication other than text.
- Irish based Team Members and Project Mangers did not consider they were part of a single virtual team and spoke in terms of the Irish team and the Far Eastern team.
- Productivity on both projects was low and deadlines were only achieved by both teams working overtime and weekends.

Ultimately these problems had repercussions for the quality of the products that were tested. This was reflected in the number of errors which were discovered after the delivery of both products.

*What are the key objectives and variables that need to be addressed to develop and facilitate GSD virtual team software testing*?
Management must be made aware that successful virtual team based software testing, is not simply a technical activity. It also has important social and cultural implications which need to be recognised. There are factors and issues which specifically impact GSD and virtual team operation which need to be acknowledged and addressed. The reality is that the technical, social and cultural aspects all have important contributions to make to ensure effective software testing takes place in a virtual team environment.

Recognition of this fact and the provision of relevant resources and support to address these issues are essential. The specific factors which this research has identified to develop and facilitate GSD virtual team software testing are outlined in Section 9.2 and presented in Figure 9.4.

*Is software testing a simple activity that can be easily offshored utilising virtual teams?*
This research clearly demonstrated that testing is not necessarily a simple activity. Where there is the need for the interdependence of tasks between locations testing is prone to suffer the same type of problems as those

which arise with other aspects of virtual team based software development. In these circumstances testing cannot be considered an easy activity to offshore utilising virtual teams.

*Is virtual team software testing different to virtual team software development and if it is how and why are these differences manifested?*
Virtual team software testing is prone to suffer the same types of problems as any other part of the virtual team based software development process. Clearly testing can be as complex and challenging and suffer the same negative forces with the same results. As this research has highlighted, all the negative factors that are inherent to a globally distributed virtual team environment came in to play and their negative impact was significant.

*What can this investigation add to the body of existing knowledge regarding globally distributed virtual team software testing and to GSD in general?*
The identification of fear and its implications for the operation of both virtual teams is an important contribution. This issue has not been considered in the literature to any great extent. This research indicates that this has been a serious omission.

This investigation has also highlighted that the universalism of the view in the literature that software testing is a simple task and can be easily offshored is not correct. If management do not understand and address the GSD and virtual team factors which can impact on testing, this can directly lead to serious consequences for the success of such projects.

## 9.4 The Contribution Made by this Research

The objective of this section is to present the findings from this research in summary form and highlight the specific contributions which have been identified from undertaking this study.

### 9.4.1. Fear

A key contribution this study has highlighted is the significant and prolonged impact fear has on those whose work was offshored. In the virtual team setting this has major implications for the successful implementation of this type of strategy. While the negative impact fear has in the GSD environment is briefly mentioned in the literature, it has not been given the prominence this research indicates it warrants.

It is recognized that the essential elements required for successful distributed software development include the establishment of trust, successful team building and effective cooperation and knowledge transfer between sites. The results from this investigation clearly demonstrate the prolonged negative impact fear had in all of these areas:

- It demotivated staff at the offshoring location.
- It inhibited team cooperation.
- It helped to foster a reluctance to share relevant knowledge with remote colleagues or/and in some cases knowledge was completely withheld.
- Was a barrier to developing trust with remote colleagues.
- Helped to develop a "them and us" culture.
- Helped to foster the belief that their remote colleagues were actively undermining the Irish based team members
- Had a negative impact on effective project management.

Of equal importance were the negative consequences of the constant use of what the researcher has termed the cost and productivity mantras: *"An Engineer is two fifths the cost in The Far East compared to Ireland. Therefore, you must be more value adding"* to motivate staff. This research clearly demonstrated the counter productive nature of the constant use of this approach.

### 9.4.2 Communication

The negative impact fear directly had on the level of communication between virtual team sites also emerged from the analysis of the data. In the virtual team context communication between locations needs to be monitored and when required steps taken to increase its efficiency. To facilitate this strategy a clearly defined and documented communication procedure should be in place, effectively implemented and its results monitored.

### 9.4.3 Virtual Teams and Software Testing

This research has highlighted that software testing is not necessarily a simple well-defined task that can be easily offshored, as the literature would suggest. Where virtual teams are established to undertake complex interdependent testing then all the negative aspects of GSD and virtual team operation come into play. In these circumstances testing is not different from any other aspect of the GSD virtual team software development process. All the negative factors which are synonymous with GSD can come into play. This must be recognised and the salient aspects of GSD and virtual team operation be understood by management and steps taken to put the structures in place to address the specific requirements of operating in this type of environment.

### 9.4.4 Informed Senior Management

The importance of Senior Management understanding the implications of implementing a global GSD strategy has been demonstrated by this research. Where an organisation decides to implement a virtual team strategy, corporate senior management require a clear knowledge of the problems as well as the benefits of implementing such an approach. This should be based on the provision of information which not only highlights the potential benefits, but also presents realistic cost and outlines the true risks involved.

It is also important for senior management to understand if the objective is to utilise labour arbitrage at a remote site and combine it on a long-term basis with the technical skills at a more costly and well-established location. This needs to be effectively communicated. This requires the organisation's continued commitment to the staff at the well-established location to be clearly articulated at a corporate level.

If, on the other hand, the objective of implementing a virtual team strategy is to simply transfer knowledge from an established location to staff at a cheaper site it has to be expected that this will be recognised and resented by the existing staff at the location that is going to be downsized. Therefore, their willingness to transfer knowledge and cooperate with this strategy will be negatively impacted.

### 9.4.5 Culture

While the importance of knowledge of remote colleagues culture is well documented in the literature, the severity of the problems experienced in this investigation are considered worthy of mention. This research has highlighted the implications of implementing a policy which was based on the fact that the Far Eastern team members would not say no when they were requested to undertake additional work. Culturally, in the Far East saying no is not an acceptable response to a request from someone in authority. As a result, at a divisional level (not the testing division) even when this problem was identified, it was decided to continue working the Far Eastern staff for as many hours as they were willing to do.

The outcome of this approach was that competent and trained Far Eastern staff left the organisation on a regular basis due to being over worked. In the view of the management of the testing department this was false economy, while productivity may have increased in the short term the cost incurred in losing and replacing trained and technically competent staff was not given due consideration.

This view was not universally held in Computing World and some other divisions continued to experience very high labour turnover as a result of implementing what was termed a 24/7 approach. This research has highlighted, there is a specific requirement for the provision of relevant cultural training for the management and virtual team members at each location.

### 9.4.6 Follow The Sun Testing

What has been termed as a *follow-the-sun* approach has been discussed at length in the literature. The reason for its inclusion here is because it has not previously been considered from the testing perspective. Given the suggestions in the GSD literature as to the straightforward nature of testing. It would not have been unreasonable to expect *a follow the sun* approach could have been employed to undertake testing on both of the projects researched. Indeed this was being extolled by Computing World management as a potential benefit of implementing the virtual software testing team strategy.

In fact the reality proved quite different. While in theory a *follow the sun* approach is very appealing, it was in more difficult to implement than expected. This was due to the complex and interdependent nature of the testing carried out. Too much time had to be spent documenting current progress to pass on to the respective team members in the Far East and vice versa, to make such an approach workable. Where success was achieved with temporal difference was when tasks could be clearly partitioned and one location or the other took complete ownership of these tasks.

### 9.4.7 Bottom-up Research Approach

The participant observational approach and the length of time spent onsite provided insightful access to the operation of the test department and the Alpha and Beta teams. They were considered from the perspectives of the Team Members, Team Leaders Project Managers and Test Manager. This bottom up approach was considered important as it provided a broad overview of what was actually taking place. The divergence of views on the importance and impact of specific issues and factors depending on the role an individual carried out was of particular interest.

## 9.5 Further Research

With specific reference to Computing World the findings from this investigation were presented to the Ireland based management. The findings have also been presented to a number of companies nationally and internationally. Based on these presentations a number of these organisations have expressed interest in assisting with further research in this area.

As this work has highlighted the importance of fear and its negative influence on the operation of virtual teams and GSD in general it clearly warrants further investigation. It is hoped this work and its publications will assist to highlight this important issue and provide a basis to facilitate others to undertake additional research on this topic or in related areas.

In addition, the impact gender has on collaboration in a GSD and specifically, a virtual team environment should be researched in more depth. This has particular implications for Western based organisations when offshoring their software development to countries which have a distinctly different attitude to gender related issues.

The researcher's objective is to take the findings from this investigation and develop them further in the areas of globally distributed software development and virtual team operation with particular emphasis on the needs of small to medium sized Irish based organisations. Specific emphasis will be placed on how these findings can be generalised to other areas of the software development processes besides testing. The important issue of how it can best be tailored to the needs of small to medium sized organisations will also be considered. The overall objective is that the results from this research can be used to make a contribution to improve the management and operation of globally distributed virtual software teams.